THE ENGLISH ASSOCIATION
BOOK OF VERSE

THE ENGLISH ASSOCIATION

(FOUNDED 1906)

President 1953/54: CHARLES MORGAN

Chairman of Committee

Instr. Rear-Admiral SIR ARTHUR HALL, K.B.E., C.B.

AIMS AND ACTIVITIES

1. To unite and introduce to one another those who are interested in English Language and Literature, whether as writers, teachers, artists, actors, or administrators; and to act as a link between groups engaged in specialized English work.

2. To uphold the standards of English writing and speech; to contribute to English letters, scholarship, and research; to discuss methods of English teaching; and to encourage especially the work of younger members.

3. To spread as widely as possible the knowledge and enjoyment of English Literature.

4. To put these aims into practice by organizing lectures, conferences, and social functions, issuing a magazine and other publications, and providing a Literary Advice Panel (for detailed particulars please apply to the Secretary).

SUBSCRIPTIONS

The *financial* year runs from 1st January to 31st December, and an ordinary subscription paid at any time during the year entitles a member to the Association's magazine ENGLISH (three issues) and the Presidential Address.

The annual subscription to the Central Body is £1 1s., or, with *Essays and Studies* (New Series) and *The Year's Work in English Studies*, £2 2s., and is due on the 1st January.

Life Membership (which does not cover the two special publications *Essays and Studies* and *The Year's Work in English Studies*) is £15 15s.

The annual subscription of branch members is fixed within certain limits by the Branch.

SCHOOLS and COLLEGES can establish a Junior branch at an all-in subscription of either £1 1s. or £2s. 2s., and can purchase additional publications at the reduced rate to members.

STUDENT membership is open on special terms to students up to the age of 23 who are interested in English Language and Literature.

Subscriptions should be made in favour of the English Association and sent to the Secretary, 8 Cromwell Place, London, S.W.7.

(*Telephone:* Kensington 8480)

The anthology has been compiled for the Association by two members of Committee: Peter Leyland, author of *The Naked Mountain and Other Poems*, and M. Alderton Pink, writer on educational and social subjects and editor of school editions of many English classics.

THE ENGLISH ASSOCIATION
BOOK OF VERSE

*An Anthology of English Poetry
of The British Isles
From Chaucer to the Present Day*

SELECTED AND ARRANGED BY
PETER LEYLAND

IN COLLABORATION WITH
M. ALDERTON PINK

London
PUBLISHED FOR THE ENGLISH ASSOCIATION
BY GEORGE ALLEN & UNWIN LTD

*Printed in Great Britain
in* 10 *point Baskerville type
by Unwin Brothers Limited
Woking and London*

PREFACE

Sir Charles Sherrington, the eminent physiologist, gave to one of his books the title, *Man on His Nature*, and the phrase might serve as a sub-title for this anthology. Unlike the best poetry of some countries, especially outside Europe, English poetry since Chaucer's time has not limited itself to certain narrow though precious areas of experience, but has fared far and wide through all the boisterousness of life, like Chaucer's own shipman: 'With many a tempest had his beard been shake.' In this book the aim has been to show man's experience through the poetry which has expressed it, and on this basis to make a representative selection of the English poetry of the British Isles, including poetry of the twentieth century.

In the first place, therefore, the book has been divided into eight sections, as follows: *Action; Love; Art; Fantasy and Symbol; Man and Nature; The Span of Life; Man and Society; Man and God*. Within each section the items have been further arranged, according to subject, feeling, and treatment, in a way which may in part be illustrated by the following brief outline of the section *Art*.

The section opens with poetry on buildings, from an early city of Arabia 'half as old as time' (an estimate not far out under Archbishop Ussher's chronology then in vogue), down to the architecture of English churches. Sculpture follows, and other plastic art, including the art of ancient Greece, in contrast with the grim northern fantasy of a bronze colossus carved in the form of Dürer's 'Melancholia'. Painting, music, and dramatic art are treated in turn by poets of various centuries, and are followed by other arts which it would not be right to omit. . . . When a woman has been (like the small girl's mother) 'attractivating herself', the results are different if described by Herrick, Pope, or Shakespeare. . . . From the point of view of the artists, there is much in art beside fulfilment, and Browning has looked at the hopes, fears, and failures which beset them. But poets in general have had much more to say about their own feelings and problems than about those of other artists, and the latter half of the section is concerned with poetry, including the comments of some poets on fellow-practitioners whom they regard as unsuccessful. Different poets, more alike in the depths than on the surface, trace the emotional and sensuous basis of their experience; describe their initiation into their profession, and its trials and sufferings; and prophesy undying life for the verse of others, if not for their own. But in the last resort poetry satisfies those who read, not those who write it, and the section ends with the sigh of Shakespeare, the 'myriad-minded', over his own narrowness:

'Desiring this man's art, and that man's scope.'

This section includes a number of very brief passages. Some of these lines, including Milton's melodious line on Athens, Shelley's lines on Greek statues, and the lines on music at night quoted successively from Shakespeare and Milton, have been felt by reputable judges to be among the finest in the language. Such lines can evidently stand by themselves in their place in the section. So also may Pope's couplet on Settle, which to Hazlitt was 'the finest piece of wit I know of'; or, in *Man and Nature*, Keats's lines on the nightingale at Bethlehem, and the following lines (especially the last three words) by Milton on an earlier nightingale. Some poets, of course, have excelled in brief passages and lines, and in *Love*, for example, the grumbling or ecstatic undertone of Donne's voice may often be heard. But in general the number of short passages which have been admitted depends mainly on the nature of the section.

Perhaps most of us have at some time enjoyed comparing similar situations or ideas in their treatment by different writers. Who would not enjoy a dream in which Blake's Tiger stands by the shore of the Indian Ocean glaring down at Melville's White Whale? The latter monster cannot enter this anthology; but many other juxtapositions have been possible. Hence, in *Love* (which in broad outline follows the course which love may take) even Drayton's imperishable sonnet on parting may gain a new interest from the contiguity of Donne's abrupt exclamation, the resignation of Browning's lover, the twentieth-century 'curtain' of Helen Spalding, and the unresigned bitterness of Tennyson's poem (which the disillusioned wife of a later poet wished

6

to have inscribed on her tombstone) and Landor's epigram with its perfectly placed word, 'colder'. Similarly, the plan of *Man and God* has made it possible for the complacent Calvinists of Browning and of Burns to speak in succession, and for the indignant outburst of Dryden's Adam and Eve to precede the more famous stanzas adapted by Fitzgerald from Omar.

Speaking of the poetry of the Old Testament, Matthew Henry remarked that 'there are shallows in which a lamb may wade, and there are depths in which an elephant may swim'. This is no less true of English poetry, and therefore of the verse included in this book. Swimming elephants can look after themselves, but the wading lamb may not be above a little help. Each section is preceded by a brief outline of its contents, and notes on historical, legendary, and other allusions will be found at the end of the book. Further, in choosing and arranging the items, and in giving explanatory titles to some of them, the use of the book in schools has throughout been borne in mind, but without (it is hoped) reducing its appeal to the general reader for whom it is primarily intended.

A poem which does not appear to have received a title from its author is normally printed without a title; or, if a title has been given for the purpose of the anthology, the first line of the poem appears in brackets after the author's name. Where an item consists of a passage as distinct from a complete poem, the word 'From' appears in its title, or (if a special title has been given to the passage) the title given by the author to the whole poem follows his name. Where use has been made within an item of 'the anthologist's time-honoured right of excision', in Mr. Norman Ault's phrase, an indication is normally given in the text.

The anthology is edited for the English Association under the aegis of the Publications Committee. In settling the titles and scope of the respective sections and in other matters, I have throughout worked in collaboration with Mr. Alderton Pink. In addition to reviewing the items with the requirements of schools in mind, Mr. Pink has furnished the notes mentioned above; and his has been the task of scrutinizing the texts of the items in order to make them accurate and authentic, and of bringing consistency into such matters as spelling, punctuation, and use of capital letters, so far as such consistency appeared to be defensible, and to be compatible with the intentions of the authors. Apart from a few poems, mainly in dialect, the spelling and punctuation have been modernized throughout.

It would not be right for me to omit from this Preface some personal acknowledgments. In particular, I should mention the debt owed to Mr. Guy Boas and to Dr. Arundell Esdaile, Chairman and ex-Chairman of the Publications Committee, in connection with the planning of the volume; to Miss V. F. Edmonds, Senior English Mistress, Wimbledon High School for Girls, for suggestions regarding the selection and arrangement of items; and to my wife, for unfailing help and for the compilation of the Index.

PETER LEYLAND

January 1953

ACKNOWLEDGMENTS

The English Association is indebted to the following authors, authors' representatives, and publishers for permission to reprint the poems and passages mentioned below: Mr. W. H. Auden and Messrs. Faber & Faber, Ltd., for the poem from *The Orators;* Messrs. Sidgwick & Jackson, Ltd., for the passage from *Collected Poems* by Rupert Brooke; Mr. Roy Campbell for a poem from *Collected Poems* (The Bodley Head) and a passage from *Talking Bronco* (Messrs. Faber & Faber, Ltd.); Mr. Walter de la Mare and Messrs. Faber & Faber, Ltd., for poems from *Collected Poems* and a passage from *The Burning-Glass*; Mr. T. S. Eliot and Messrs. Faber & Faber, Ltd., for the poem and passages from *Collected Poems*; Mrs. J. E. Flecker and Messrs. William Heinemann, Ltd., for the passage from *Hassan*, by James Elroy Flecker; the Trustees of the Hardy Estate and Messrs. Macmillan & Co., Ltd., for poems from *Collected Poems of Thomas Hardy*; the Oxford University Press for poems from *Poems of Gerard Manley Hopkins*; The Society of Authors as the literary representative of the Trustees of the Estate of the late A. E. Housman, and Messrs. Jonathan Cape, Ltd., for poems from *Collected Poems*; Messrs. Routledge & Kegan Paul, Ltd., for lines from *Collected Poems of Sidney Keyes*; Mrs. Bambridge, Messrs. Macmillan & Co., Ltd., and the Macmillan Company of Canada, for *The Way through the Woods* from Rudyard Kipling's *Rewards and Fairies*; Professor C. Day Lewis and the Hogarth Press, Ltd., for the poem and passages from *Collected Poems*; Dr. John Masefield, O.M., The Society of Authors, and the Macmillan Company, New York, for the poem from *Collected Poems* (Messrs. William Heinemann, Ltd.); the author's executor and Messrs. Constable & Co., Ltd., for poems from *Poetical Works of George Meredith*; Sir Francis Meynell and Messrs. Burns Oates & Washburn, Ltd., for poems by Alice Meynell and Francis Thompson; the author's executors and Messrs. Chatto & Windus, Ltd., for the poem from *The Poems of Wilfred Owen*; Messrs. John Lane The Bodley Head, Ltd., for the poem from *Poems* by Stephen Phillips; Mr. Diarmuid Russell for lines from *Collected Poems* by George William Russell (AE); The Hon. Victoria Sackville-West and the Hogarth Press, Ltd., for the poem from *Collected Poems*; Mr. Siegfried Sassoon and Messrs. Faber & Faber, Ltd., for the poem from *The Heart's Journey*; Miss Helen Spalding and Messrs. Methuen & Co., Ltd., for the passage from *No Images Return*; Mr. Stephen Spender and Messrs. Faber & Faber, Ltd., for the poem from *Poems*; Messrs. William Heinemann, Ltd., for passages from Swinburne's *Collected Poetical Works*; Mr. Dylan Thomas and Messrs. J. M. Dent & Sons, Ltd., for the passage from *Deaths and Entrances*; Mrs. Helen Thomas for the poem from *Collected Poems* by Edward Thomas (Messrs. Faber & Faber, Ltd.); Messrs. George Harrap & Co., Ltd., for poems from *Poems of Sir William Watson, 1878–1935*; Mrs. W. B. Yeats and Messrs. Macmillan & Co., Ltd., for poems from *Collected Poems of William Butler Yeats*; and Dr. Andrew Young and Messrs. Jonathan Cape, Ltd., for poems from *Collected Poems of Andrew Young*.

Mr. G. Winthrop Young has been so good as to provide an authentic text of the anonymous lines (which may be by an American author) printed as item 24.

CONTENTS

I
ACTION

In this section we see men and women enjoying the movement and energy of their bodies, or undergoing failure and pain, often under the dominance of some purpose hardly capable of achievement, and certainly incapable of any easy achievement. In myth and metaphor, or in terms of magic, man has imagined flight through 'the shoreless air', by day or night, until in our own day poets have been able to write of actual flight. At sea at all times we find ships struggling with storms, losing men overboard, caught in the ice of high latitudes, or becalmed in the tropics; and war at sea brings further perils. On sea and land alike, it has been man's nature to seek, for the sake of what he may find, or perhaps merely for the sake of seeking. Less remote and arduous, the physical pleasure of sport or of dancing is described. Woman is seen acting like man or in her own way, or as urging or luring man to action. Man has made a profession of arms, and knights and soldiers express their code, reveal their character, exult in conflict, or endure overthrow with patience or with indignation. After violent action may follow thoughts of ease and rest. Action again may be seen from the point of view of those who do not act but are acted upon, and perhaps must endure protracted suffering or be killed. Finally, death is seen as the general end of action of every kind, or as a portal to new action.

I   From *Saul*

Oh, our manhood's prime vigour! no spirit feels waste,
Not a muscle is stopped in its playing, nor sinew unbraced.
Oh, the wild joys of living! the leaping from rock up to
        rock—
The strong rending of boughs from the fir-tree,—the cool
        silver shock
Of the plunge in a pool's living water,—the hunt of the
        bear,
And the sultriness showing the lion is couched in his lair.

And the meal—the rich dates yellowed over with gold dust
    divine,
And the locust's-flesh steeped in the pitcher! the full
    draught of wine,
And the sleep in the dried river-channel where bulrushes
    tell
That the water was wont to go warbling so softly and well.
How good is man's life, the mere living! how fit to employ
All the heart and the soul and the senses, for ever in joy!

ROBERT BROWNING

2

Hey nonny no!
Men are fools that wish to die!
Is't not fine to dance and sing
When the bells of death do ring?
Is't not fine to swim in wine,
And turn upon the toe
And sing hey nonny no,
When the winds blow and the seas flow?
Hey nonny no!

ANONYMOUS (17th century)

3

What glory is there in a common good
That hangs for every peasant to achieve?
That like I best, that flies beyond my reach.
Set me to scale the high Pyramides
And thereon set the diadem of France,
I'll either rend it with my nails to naught,
Or mount the top with my aspiring wings
Although my downfall be the deepest hell.

CHRISTOPHER MARLOWE
(The Massacre at Paris, II)

4

These were tame pleasures. She would often climb
    The steepest ladder of the crudded rack
Up to some beakèd cape of cloud sublime,
    And like Arion on the dolphin's back
Ride singing through the shoreless air. Oft-time,
    Following the serpent lightning's winding track,
She ran upon the platforms of the wind,
And laughed to hear the fireballs roar behind.

PERCY BYSSHE SHELLEY

(*The Witch of Atlas*)

5

O, what a dainty pleasure 'tis
To ride in the air
When the moon shines fair,
And sing, and dance, and toy, and kiss!
Over woods, high rocks, and mountains,
Over seas, our mistress' fountains,
Over steeples, towers, and turrets,
We fly by night, 'mongst troops of spirits.
No ring of bells to our ear sounds,
No howls of wolves, no yelps of hounds;
No, not the noise of water's breach,
Or cannon's throat, our height can reach.

THOMAS MIDDLETON (*The Witch*, *III*, *3*)

6   *Lucifer in Starlight*

On a starred night Prince Lucifer uprose.
Tired of his dark dominion swung the fiend
Above the rolling ball in cloud part screened,
Where sinners hugged their spectre of repose.
Poor prey to his hot fit of pride were those.
And now upon his western wing he leaned,
Now his huge bulk o'er Afric's sands careened,
Now the black planet shadowed Arctic snows.

Soaring through wider zones that pricked his scars
With memory of the old revolt from Awe,
He reached a middle height, and at the stars,
Which are the brain of heaven, he looked, and sank.
Around the ancient track marched, rank on rank,
The army of unalterable law.

GEORGE MEREDITH

7

Looking upon proud Phaeton wrapped in fire,
The gentle queen did much bewail his fall;
But Mortimer commended his desire
To lose one poor life or to govern all.
'What though', quoth he, 'he madly did aspire
And his great mind made him proud Fortune's thrall?
Yet, in despite when she her worst had done,
He perished in the chariot of the sun.'

MICHAEL DRAYTON (The Barons' Wars)

8   *An Irish Airman Foresees His Death*

I know that I shall meet my fate
Somewhere among the clouds above;
Those that I fight I do not hate,
Those that I guard I do not love;
My country is Kiltartan Cross,
My countrymen Kiltartan's poor,
No likely end could bring them loss
Or leave them happier than before.
Nor law, nor duty bade me fight,
Nor public men, nor cheering crowds,
A lonely impulse of delight
Drove to this tumult in the clouds;
I balanced all, brought all to mind,
The years to come seemed waste of breath,
A waste of breath the years behind
In balance with this life, this death.

WILLIAM BUTLER YEATS

One silver-white and one of scarlet hue,
Storm hornets humming in the wind of death,
Two aeroplanes were fighting in the blue
Above our town; and if I held my breath,
It was because my youth was in the Red
While in the White an unknown pilot flew—
And that the White had risen overhead.

From time to time the crackle of a gun
Far into flawless ether faintly railed,
And now, mosquito-thin, into the Sun,
And now like mating dragonflies they sailed:
And, when like eagles near the earth they drove,
The Red, still losing what the White had won,
The harder for each lost advantage strove.

So lovely lay the land—the towers and trees
Taking the seaward counsel of the stream:
The city seemed, above the far-off seas,
The crest and turret of a Jacob's dream,
And those two gun-birds in their frantic spire
At death-grips for its ultimate regime—
Less to be whirled by anger than desire.

Till (Glory!) from his chrysalis of steel
The Red flung wide the fatal fans of fire:
I saw the long flames ribboning, unreel,
And slow bitumen trawling from his pyre.
I knew the ecstasy, the fearful throes,
And the white phoenix from his scarlet sire
As silver in the Solitude he rose.

The towers and trees were lifted hymns of praise,
The city was a prayer, the land a nun:
The noonday azure strumming all its rays
Sang that a famous battle had been won,
As signing his white Cross, the very Sun,
The Solar Christ and captain of my days
Zoomed to the zenith; and his will was done.

                              ROY CAMPBELL

If thou wouldst know thy maker, search the seas.

THOMAS DEKKER (*The Double PP*)

11   *Sir Patrick Spens*

The king sits in Dumferling town,
    Drinking the blood-red wine:
'O whar will I get guid sailòr,
    To sail this ship of mine?'

Up and spake an eldern knight,
    Sat at the king's right knee:
'Sir Patrick Spens is the best sailòr,
    That sails upon the sea.'

The king has written a braid letter,
    And signed it wi' his hand;
And sent it to Sir Patrick Spens,
    Was walking on the sand.

The first line that Sir Patrick read,
    A loud laugh laughed he:
The next line that Sir Patrick read,
    The tear blinded his e'e.

'O wha is this has done this deed,
    This ill deed done to me;
To send me out this time o' the year,
    To sail upon the sea?

'Make haste, make haste, my merry men all,
    Our good ship sails the morn.'
'O say na sae, my master dear,
    For I fear a deadly storm.

'Late late yestreen I saw the new moon
    Wi' the auld moon in hir arme;
And I fear, I fear, my dear master,
    That we will come to harm.'

O our Scots nobles wer right laith
    To wet their cork-heel'd schoon;
But lang owre a' the play were played,
    Their hats they swam aboon.

O lang, lang, may the ladies sit
    Wi' their fans into their hand,
Or e'er they see Sir Patrick Spens
    Come sailing to the land.

O lang, lang, may the ladies stand
    Wi' thair gold kems in their hair,
Waiting for their ain dear lords,
    For they'll see them na mair.

Haf owre, haf owre to Aberdour,
    It's fifty fathom deep:
And there lies guid Sir Patrick Spens,
    Wi' the Scots lords at his feet.

ANONYMOUS

12   *The Convergence of the Twain*

(*Lines on the Loss of the 'Titanic'*)

In a solitude of the sea
Deep from human vanity,
And the Pride of Life that planned her, stilly couches she.

Steel chambers, late the pyres
Of her salamandrine fires,
Cold currents thrid, and turn to rhythmic tidal lyres.

Over the mirrors meant
To glass the opulent
The sea-worm crawls—grotesque, slimed, dumb, indifferent.

Jewels in joy designed
To ravish the sensuous mind
Lie lightless, all their sparkles bleared and black and blind.

Dim moon-eyed fishes near
Gaze at the gilded gear
And query: 'What does this vaingloriousness down here?' . . .

19

Well: while was fashioning
This creature of cleaving wing,
The Immanent Will that stirs and urges everything

Prepared a sinister mate
For her—so gaily great—
A Shape of Ice, for the time far and dissociate.

And as the smart ship grew
In stature, grace, and hue,
In shadowy silent distance grew the Iceberg too.

Alien they seemed to be:
No mortal eye could see
The intimate welding of their later history,

Or sign that they were bent
By paths coincident
On being anon twin halves of one august event,

Till the Spinner of the Years
Said 'Now!' And each one hears,
And consummation comes, and jars two hemispheres.

THOMAS HARDY

13 *The Castaway*

Obscurest night involv'd the sky,
   The Atlantic billows roar'd,
When such a destin'd wretch as I,
   Wash'd headlong from on board,
Of friends, of hope, of all bereft,
His floating home for ever left. . . .

Not long beneath the whelming brine,
   Expert to swim, he lay;
Nor soon he felt his strength decline,
   Or courage die away;
But wag'd with death a lasting strife,
Supported by despair of life.

He shouted: nor his friends had fail'd
    To check the vessel's course,
But so the furious blast prevail'd,
    That, pitiless perforce,
They left their outcast mate behind,
And scudded still before the wind.

Some succour yet they could afford;
    And, such as storms allow,
The cask, the coop, the floated cord,
    Delayed not to bestow.
But he, they knew, nor ship nor shore,
Whate'er they gave, should visit more. . . .

At length, his transient respite past,
    His comrades, who before
Had heard his voice in ev'ry blast,
    Could catch the sound no more:
For then, by toil subdued, he drank
The stifling wave, and then he sank.

No poet wept him: but the page
    Of narrative sincere,
That tells his name, his worth, his age,
    Is wet with Anson's tear.
And tears by bards or heroes shed
Alike immortalize the dead.

I therefore purpose not, or dream,
    Descanting on his fate,
To give the melancholy theme
    A more enduring date:
But misery still delights to trace
Its semblance in another's case.

No voice divine the storm allay'd,
    No light propitious shone;
When, snatch'd from all effectual aid,
    We perish'd, each alone:
But I beneath a rougher sea,
And whelm'd in deeper gulfs than he.

WILLIAM COWPER

And now the Storm-blast came, and he
Was tyrannous and strong:
He struck with his o'ertaking wings,
And chased us south along.

With sloping masts and dipping prow,
As who pursued with yell and blow
Still treads the shadow of his foe,
And forward bends his head,
The ship drove fast, loud roared the blast,
And southward aye we fled.

And now there came both mist and snow,
And it grew wondrous cold:
And ice, mast-high, came floating by,
As green as emerald.

And through the drifts the snowy clifts
Did send a dismal sheen:
Nor shapes of men nor beasts we ken—
The ice was all between.

The ice was here, the ice was there,
The ice was all around:
It cracked and growled, and roared and howled,
Like noises in a swound!

At length did cross an Albatross,
Through the fog it came;
As if it had been a Christian soul,
We hailed it in God's name.

It ate the food it ne'er had eat,
And round and round it flew.
The ice did split with a thunder-fit;
The helmsman steered us through!

. . . .

The fair breeze blew, the white foam flew,
The furrow followed free;

We were the first that ever burst
Into that silent sea.

Down dropt the breeze, the sails dropt down,
'Twas sad as sad could be;
And we did speak only to break
The silence of the sea!

All in a hot and copper sky,
The bloody Sun, at noon,
Right up above the mast did stand,
No bigger than the Moon.

Day after day, day after day,
We stuck, nor breath nor motion;
As idle as a painted ship
Upon a painted ocean.

Water, water, everywhere,
And all the boards did shrink;
Water, water everywhere
Nor any drop to drink.

SAMUEL TAYLOR COLERIDGE

15   From *The Revenge*

And they mann'd the Revenge with a swarthier alien crew,
And away she sail'd with her loss and long'd for her own;
When a wind from the lands they had ruin'd awoke from
    sleep,
And the water began to heave and the weather to moan,
And or ever that evening ended a great gale blew,
And a wave like the wave that is raised by an earthquake
    grew,
Till it smote on their hulls and their sails and their masts
    and their flags,
And the whole sea plunged and fell on the shot-shatter'd
    navy of Spain,

And the little Revenge herself went down by the island
   crags
To be lost evermore in the main.

ALFRED, LORD TENNYSON

16   The Battle of the Baltic

Of Nelson and the North
Sing the glorious day's renown,
When to battle fierce came forth
All the might of Denmark's crown,
And her arms along the deep proudly shone,—
By each gun the lighted brand
In a bold determined hand;
And the Prince of all the land
Led them on.

Like leviathans afloat
Lay their bulwarks on the brine,
While the sign of battle flew
On the lofty British line:
It was ten of April morn by the chime:
As they drifted on their path
There was silence deep as death,
And the boldest held his breath
For a time.

But the might of England flushed
To anticipate the scene;
And her van the fleeter rushed
O'er the deadly space between.
'Hearts of oak!' our captain cried; when each gun
From its adamantine lips
Spread a death-shade round the ships,
Like the hurricane eclipse
Of the sun.

Again! again! again!
And the havoc did not slack,
Till a feeble cheer the Dane,

To our cheering sent us back:
Their shots along the deep slowly boom;
Then ceased—and all is wail
As they strike the shattered sail,
Or, in conflagration pale,
Light the gloom.

Out spoke the victor then,
As he hailed them o'er the wave,
'Ye are brothers! ye are men!
And we conquer but to save;
So peace instead of death let us bring:
But yield, proud foe, thy fleet
With the crews at England's feet,
And make submission meet
To our King.' . . .

Now joy, old England, raise!
For the tidings of thy might,
By the festal cities' blaze,
Whilst the wine-cup shines in light!
And yet amidst that joy and uproar,
Let us think of them that sleep
Full many a fathom deep,
By thy wild and stormy steep,
Elsinore!

THOMAS CAMPBELL

17   *Zeus and the Greek Ships at Troy*

The splendour of the burning ships might satiate his eyes.

GEORGE CHAPMAN (HOMER'S *Iliad*)

18   *Ulysses*

It little profits that an idle king,
By this still hearth, among these barren crags,
Match'd with an aged wife, I mete and dole
Unequal laws unto a savage race,

That hoard, and sleep, and feed, and know not me.
I cannot rest from travel; I will drink
Life to the lees. All times I have enjoyed
Greatly, have suffered greatly, both with those
That love me, and alone; on shore, and when
Thro' scudding drifts the rainy Hyades
Vext the dim sea. I am become a name:
For always roaming with a hungry heart
Much have I seen and known,—cities of men
And manners, climates, councils, governments,
Myself not least, but honour'd of them all,—
And drunk delight of battle with my peers,
Far on the ringing plains of windy Troy.
I am a part of all that I have met;
Yet all experience is an arch wherethro'
Gleams that untravell'd world, whose margin fades
For ever and for ever when I move.
How dull it is to pause, to make an end,
To rust unburnish'd, not to shine in use!
As though to breathe were life! Life piled on life
Were all too little, and of one to me
Little remains; but every hour is saved
From that eternal silence, something more,
A bringer of new things, and vile it were
For some three suns to store and hoard myself,
And this gray spirit yearning in desire
To follow knowledge like a sinking star,
Beyond the utmost bound of human thought.

This is my son, mine own Telemachus,
To whom I leave the sceptre and the isle,—
Well-loved of me, discerning to fulfil
This labour, by slow prudence to make mild
A rugged people, and through soft degrees
Subdue them to the useful and the good.
Most blameless is he, centred in the sphere
Of common duties, decent not to fail
In offices of tenderness, and pay
Meet adoration to my household gods,
When I am gone. He works his work, I mine.

There lies the port; the vessel puffs her sail;
There gloom the dark, broad seas. My mariners,

Souls that have toil'd, and wrought, and thought with me—
That ever with a frolic welcome took
The thunder and the sunshine, and opposed
Free hearts, free foreheads—you and I are old;
Old age hath yet his honour and his toil.
Death closes all; but something ere the end,
Some work of noble note, may yet be done,
Not unbecoming men that strove with Gods.
The lights begin to twinkle from the rocks;
The long day wanes; the slow moon climbs; the deep
Moans round with many voices. Come, my friends,
'Tis not too late to seek a newer world.
Push off, and sitting well in order smite
The sounding furrows; for my purpose holds
To sail beyond the sunset, and the baths
Of all the western stars, until I die.
It may be that the gulfs will wash us down;
It may be we shall touch the Happy Isles,
And see the great Achilles, whom we knew.
Tho' much is taken, much abides; and tho'
We are not now that strength which in old days
Moved earth and heaven, that which we are, we are,—
One equal temper of heroic hearts,
Made weak by time and fate, but strong in will
To strive, to seek, to find, and not to yield.

ALFRED, LORD TENNYSON

19   From *Hassan*

We are the Pilgrims, master; we shall go
    Always a little further: it may be
Beyond that last blue mountain barred with snow,
    Across that angry or that glimmering sea,
White on a throne or guarded in a cave
    There lives a prophet who can understand
Why men were born: but surely we are brave,
    Who make the Golden Journey to Samarkand.

JAMES ELROY FLECKER

Breathed hot
From all the boundless furnace of the sky,
And the wide glittering waste of burning sand,
A suffocating wind the pilgrim smites
With instant death. Patient of thirst and toil,
Son of the desert! even the camel feels,
Shot through his withered heart, the fiery blast.
Or from the black-red ether, bursting broad,
Sallies the sudden whirlwind. Straight the sands,
Commoved around, in gathering eddies play:
Nearer and nearer, still they darkening come;
Till, with the general all-involving storm
Swept up, the whole continuous wilds arise;
And by their noon-day fount dejected thrown
Or sunk at night in sad disastrous sleep,
Beneath descending hills, the caravan
Is buried deep. In Cairo's crowded streets
The impatient merchant, wondering, waits in vain,
And Mecca saddens at the long delay.

JAMES THOMSON (*The Seasons*)

21

Nurse, O! my love is slain: I saw him go
O'er the white Alps, alone.

JOHN DONNE (*Elegy* XVI)

22 *Atalanta*

Me the snows
That face the first o' the morning, and cold hills
Full of the land-wind and sea-travelling storms
And many a wandering wing of noisy nights
That know the thunder and hear the thickening wolves—
Me the utmost pine and footless frost of woods
That talk with many winds and gods, the hours
Re-risen, and white divisions of the dawn,

Springs thousand-tongued with the intermitting reed
And streams that murmur of the mother snow—
Me these allure, and know me.

ALGERNON CHARLES SWINBURNE (*Atalanta in Calydon*)

23

Great things are done when men and mountains meet;
This is not done by jostling in the street.

WILLIAM BLAKE

24

Change was his mistress, Chance his councillor,
 Love could not hold him, Duty forged no chain;
The wide seas and the mountains called to him,
 And grey dawns saw his camp-fire in the rain.

ANONYMOUS

25 From *A Hunting Song*

The dusky night rides down the sky,
 And ushers in the morn;
The hounds all join in glorious cry,
 The huntsman winds his horn,
  And a-hunting we will go.

HENRY FIELDING

26

Meanwhile, welcome joy and feast,
Midnight shout, and revelry,
Tipsy dance, and jollity.
Braid your locks with rosy twine,
Dropping odours, dropping wine.
Rigour now is gone to bed,

And Advice with scrupulous head,
Strict Age, and sour Severity,
With their grave saws in slumber lie.
We that are of purer fire
Imitate the starry choir,
Who in their nightly watchful spheres
Lead in swift round the months and years.
The sounds and seas with all their finny drove
Now to the moon in wavering morris move,
And on the tawny sands and shelves
Trip the pert fairies and the dapper elves;
By dimpled brook and fountain brim
The wood nymphs decked with daisies trim
Their merry wakes and pastimes keep:
What hath night to do with sleep?

JOHN MILTON (*Comus*)

27 *Florizel to Perdita*

When you do dance, I wish you
A wave o' the sea, that you might ever do
Nothing but that.

WILLIAM SHAKESPEARE (*A Winter's Tale*, IV, 3)

28 *At Lord's*

It is little I repair to the matches of the Southron folk,
   Though my own red roses there may blow;
It is little I repair to the matches of the Southron folk,
   Though the red roses crest the caps, I know.
For the field is full of shades as I near the shadowy coast,
And a ghostly batsman plays to the bowling of a ghost,
And I look through my tears on a soundless-clapping host
   As the run-stealers flicker to and fro,
       To and fro:—
O my Hornby and my Barlow long ago!

FRANCIS THOMPSON

Releas'd from the noise of the butcher and baker
Who, my old friends be thanked, did seldom forsake her,
And from the soft duns of my landlord the Quaker,

From chiding the footmen and watching the lasses,
From Nell that burn'd milk, and Tom that broke glasses
(Sad mischiefs thro' which a good housekeeper passes!)

From some real care but more fancied vexation,
From a life parti-colour'd half reason half passion,
Here lies after all the best wench in the nation. . . .

Thus still whilst her morning unseen fled away
In ord'ring the linen and making the tea
That she scarce could have time for the psalms of the day;

And while after dinner the night came so soon
That half she propos'd very seldom was done;
With twenty God bless me's, how this day is gone!—

While she read and accounted and paid and abated,
Eat and drank, play'd and work'd, laugh'd and cried, lov'd
    and hated,
As answer'd the end of her being created:

In the midst of her age came a cruel disease
Which neither her juleps nor receipts could appease;
So down dropp'd her clay—may her Soul be at peace! . . .

Tread soft on her grave, and do right to her honour,
Let neither rude hand nor ill tongue light upon her,
Do all the small favours that now can be done her.

MATTHEW PRIOR

30   *No Second Troy*

Why should I blame her that she filled my days
With misery, or that she would of late
Have taught to ignorant men most violent ways,

Or hurled the little streets upon the great,
Had they but courage equal to desire?
What could have made her peaceful with a mind
That nobleness made simple as a fire,
With beauty like a tightened bow, a kind
That is not natural in an age like this,
Being high and solitary and most stern?
Why, what could she have done, being what she is?
Was there another Troy for her to burn?

WILLIAM BUTLER YEATS

31 *The Wandering Knight's Song*

My ornaments are arms,
My pastime is in war,
My bed is cold upon the wold,
My lamp yon star.

My journeyings are long,
My slumber short and broken;
From hill to hill I wander still,
Kissing thy token.

I ride from land to land,
I sail from sea to sea;
Some day more kind I fate may find,
Some night kiss thee.

JOHN GIBSON LOCKHART

32 *Sir Guyon Explores the Cave of Mammon*

Both roof, and floor, and walls, were all of gold,
But overgrown with dust and old decay,
And hid in darkness, that none could behold
The hue thereof; for view of cheerful day
Did never in that house itself display,
But a faint shadow of uncertain light:
Such as a lamp, whose life does fade away,
Or as the Moon, clothèd with cloudy night,
Does show to him that walks in fear and sad
    affright. . . .

Then Mammon, turning to that warrior, said;
'Lo! here the worldë's bliss: lo! here the end,
To which all men do aim, rich to be made:
Such grace now to be happy is before thee laid.'

'Certes,' (said he) 'I n'ill thine offered grace,
Ne to be made so happy do intend:
Another bliss before my eyes I place,
Another happiness, another end.
To them that list these base regards I lend;
But I in arms, and in achievements brave,
Do rather choose my flitting hours to spend,
And to be Lord of those that riches have,
Than them to have myself, and be their servile slave.'

EDMUND SPENSER (*The Faery Queen*, II, 7)

33 *Hamlet Sees the Army of Fortinbras Marching*

                    Examples gross as earth exhort me:
Witness this army of such mass and charge
Led by a delicate and tender prince,
Whose spirit with divine ambition puff'd
Makes mouths at the invisible event,
Exposing what is mortal and unsure
To all that fortune, death, and danger dare,
Even for an egg-shell. Rightly to be great
Is not to stir without great argument,
But greatly to find quarrel in a straw
When honour's at the stake. How stand I then,
That have a father kill'd, a mother stain'd,
Excitements of my reason and my blood,
And let all sleep? while, to my shame, I see
The imminent death of twenty thousand men,
That, for a fantasy and trick of fame,
Go to their graves like beds, fight for a plot
Whereon the numbers cannot try the cause,
Which is not tomb enough and continent
To hide the slain?

WILLIAM SHAKESPEARE (*Hamlet*, IV, 4)

34 *Epitaph on an Army of Mercenaries*

These, in the day when heaven was falling,
   The hour when earth's foundations fled,
Followed their mercenary calling
   And took their wages and are dead.

Their shoulders held the sky suspended;
   They stood, and earth's foundations stay;
What God abandoned, these defended,
   And saved the sum of things for pay.

ALFRED EDWARD HOUSMAN

35   *The Battle of Flodden*

But as they left the dark'ning heath,
More desperate grew the strife of death.
The English shafts in volleys hail'd,
In headlong charge their horse assail'd;
Front, flank, and rear, the squadrons sweep
To break the Scottish circle deep,
   That fought around their King.
But yet, though thick the shafts as snow,
Though charging knights like whirlwinds go,
Though bill-men ply the ghastly blow,
   Unbroken was the ring;
The stubborn spear-men still made good
Their dark impenetrable wood,
Each stepping where his comrade stood,
   The instant that he fell.
No thought was there of dastard flight;
Link'd in the serried phalanx tight,
Groom fought like noble, squire like knight,
   As fearlessly and well;
Till utter darkness closed her wing
O'er their thin host and wounded King.

SIR WALTER SCOTT (*Marmion*)

From *The Colloquy of The Sphinx and the Soldier*

(*After the Battle of El Alamein*)

Yes, you may laugh! but in an hour,
Gay as the bee to seek the flower,
Across the sands a bullet sings:
Your comrade falls: and from the spot,
Flushed like a sandgrouse by the shot,
An angel whirrs on startled wings.

Go now: tread lightly: mind the wire:
This life's as beautiful as fire
But always fighting at the bit.
Each moment is too deep to ponder
And swifter than the star that, yonder,
Slid from your sight, as soon as lit.

ROY CAMPBELL

37   *Strange Meeting*

It seemed that out of battle I escaped
Down some profound dull tunnel, long since scooped
Through granites which titanic wars had groined.
Yet also there encumbered sleepers groaned,
Too fast in thought or death to be bestirred.
Then, as I probed them, one sprang up, and stared
With piteous recognition in fixed eyes,
Lifting distressful hands as if to bless.
And by his smile, I knew that sullen hall,
By his dead smile I knew we stood in Hell.
With a thousand pains that vision's face was grained;
Yet no blood reached there from the upper ground,
And no guns thumped, or down the flues made moan.
'Strange friend,' I said, 'here is no cause to mourn.'
'None,' said the other, 'save the undone years,
The hopelessness. Whatever hope is yours,
Was my life also; I went hunting wild
After the wildest beauty in the world,

Which lies not calm in eyes, or braided hair,
But mocks the steady running of the hour,
And if it grieves, grieves richlier than here.
For by my glee might many men have laughed,
And of my weeping something had been left,
Which must die now. I mean the truth untold,
The pity of war, the pity war distilled.
Now men will go content with what we spoiled.
Or, discontent, boil bloody, and be spilled.
They will be swift with swiftness of the tigress,
None will break ranks, though nations trek from
  progress.
Courage was mine, and I had mystery,
Wisdom was mine, and I had mastery;
To miss the march of this retreating world
Into vain citadels that are not walled.
Then, when much blood had clogged their chariot-
  wheels
I would go up and wash them from sweet wells,
Even with truths that lie too deep for taint.
I would have poured my spirit without stint
But not through wounds; not on the cess of war.
Foreheads of men have bled where no wounds were.
I am the enemy you killed, my friend.
I knew you in this dark; for so you frowned
Yesterday through me as you jabbed and killed.
I parried; but my hands were loath and cold.
Let us sleep now. . . .'

WILFRID OWEN

38 *The King Kills a Sleeping Sentry*

I leave him, as I found him, fit to keep
The silent doors of everlasting sleep.

SIR JOHN BEAUMONT (Bosworth Field)

39 *The Siren to Ulysses*

Come, worthy Greek, Ulysses, come,
   Possess these shores with me;
The winds and seas are troublesome,
   And here we may be free.
Here may we sit and view their toil
   That travail in the deep,
And joy the day in mirth the while,
   And spend the night in sleep.

.   .   .   .

Who may disport them diversely
   Find never tedious day,
And ease may have variety
   As well as action may.

SAMUEL DANIEL
(*Ulysses and the Siren*)

40 From *The Lotos-Eaters*

We have had enough of action, and of motion we,
Roll'd to starboard, roll'd to larboard, when the surge was
   seething free,
Where the wallowing monster spouted his foam-fountains
   in the sea.
Let us swear an oath, and keep it with an equal mind,
In the hollow Lotos-land to live and lie reclined
On the hills like Gods together, careless of mankind.
For they lie beside their nectar, and the bolts are hurl'd
Far below them in the valleys, and the clouds are lightly
   curl'd
Round their golden houses, girdled with the gleaming
   world:
Where they smile in secret, looking over wasted lands,
Blight and famine, plague and earthquake, roaring deeps
   and fiery sands,
Clanging fights, and flaming towns, and sinking ships, and
   praying hands.

But they smile, they find a music centred in a doleful song
Steaming up, a lamentation and an ancient tale of wrong,
Like a tale of little meaning tho' the words are strong;
Chanted from an ill-used race of men that cleave the soil,
Sow the seed, and reap the harvest with enduring toil,
Storing yearly little dues of wheat, and wine and oil;
Till they perish and they suffer—some, 'tis whisper'd—
    down in hell
Suffer endless anguish, others in Elysian valleys dwell,
Resting weary limbs at last on beds of asphodel.
Surely, surely, slumber is more sweet than toil, the shore
Than labour in the deep mid-ocean, wind and wave and oar;
Oh rest ye, brother mariners, we will not wander more.

ALFRED, LORD TENNYSON

41

Action is transitory—a step, a blow,
The motion of a muscle—this way or that—
'Tis done, and in the after-vacancy
We wonder at ourselves like men betrayed:
Suffering is permanent, obscure and dark,
And shares the nature of infinity.

WILLIAM WORDSWORTH
(*The Borderers, III*)

42   *Edward the Second, in Prison, Receives*
His Murderers

This dungeon where they keep me is the sink
Wherein the filth of all the castle falls.
And there in mire and puddle have I stood
This ten days' space; and, lest that I should sleep,
One plays continually upon a drum.
They give me bread and water, being a king;
So that, for want of sleep and sustenance,
My mind's distemper'd, and my body's numbed,
And whether I have limbs or no I know not.

38

O, would my blood dropp'd out from every vein,
As doth this water from my tatter'd robes.
Tell Isabel, the queen, I look'd not thus,
When for her sake I ran at tilt in France,
And there unhors'd the Duke of Cleremont. . . .
One jewel have I left; receive thou this.
Still fear I, and I know not what's the cause,
But every joint shakes as I give it thee.
O, if thou harbour'st murder in thy heart,
Let this gift change thy mind, and save thy soul!
Know that I am a king: O, at that name
I feel a hell of grief! where is my crown?
Gone, gone! and do I still remain alive? . . .
Something still buzzeth in mine ears,
And tells me, if I sleep, I never wake.

CHRISTOPHER MARLOWE
(*Edward the Second*, V, 5)

43   *Duncan Murdered*

After life's fitful fever he sleeps well.

WILLIAM SHAKESPEARE
(*Macbeth*, III, 2)

44

Sleep after toil, port after stormy seas,
Ease after war, death after life, does greatly please.

EDMUND SPENSER
(*The Faery Queen*, I, 9)

45   *Lines for the Cenotaph to Sir John Franklin in Westminster Abbey*

Not here! the white North has thy bones; and thou,
    Heroic sailor-soul,
Art passing on thine happier voyage now
    Toward no earthly pole.

ALFRED, LORD TENNYSON

If this life-saving rock should fail
Yielding too much to my embrace
And rock and I to death should race,
The rock would stay there in the dale
While I, breaking my fall,
Would still go on
Further than any wandering star has gone.

ANDREW YOUNG

2
LOVE

After some general lines (47–54) the section follows the course which love may take from its birth to the death of the second of two lovers long afterwards, subject however to all that may interrupt such a course for a while or for ever. The flux and variety forbid any brief outline, but some groups or sequences of poems may be distinguished. Thus, we find descriptions or hints of the beauty—or otherwise—of the man or the woman (59–65); masculine complaints of the unreasonableness of 'the eternal enemy of the absolute' (73–76); rejection and parting (77–85); the death of a loved one in the early time of love (88–91); the consummation of love (95–102); separation from various causes, renunciation, or a refusal to renounce (105–115); and the continuance of love until death, or perhaps beyond death.

47

Love still has something of the sea
From whence his mother rose.
            SIR CHARLES SEDLEY (*Song*)

48

It is the pulse by which we know
Whether our souls have life or no.

                        RICHARD FLECKNOE

49

But you are wise;
Or else you love not; for to be wise and love
Exceeds man's might; that dwells with gods above.

                WILLIAM SHAKESPEARE
                        (*Troilus and Cressida*, III, 2)

Alas! alas! that ever love was sin!

GEOFFREY CHAUCER

(*The Wife of Bath's Prologue*)

51

Love's very pain is sweet,
But its reward is in the world divine
Which, if not here, it builds beyond the grave.

PERCY BYSSHE SHELLEY (*Epipsychidion*)

52

No life hath love in such sweet state as this;
No essence is so dear to moody sense,
As flesh and blood, whose quintessence is sense.
Beauty, composed of blood and flesh, moves more,
And is more plausible to blood and flesh,
Than spiritual beauty can be to the spirit.

BEN JONSON (*The Poetaster, IV*, 6)

53

Fain would I change that note
    To which fond love hath charmed me.
Long, long to sing by rote,
    Fancying that that harmed me.
Yet when this thought doth come,
'Love is the perfect sum
    Of all delight,'
I have no other choice
Either for pen or voice
    To sing or write.

O Love, they wrong thee much
    That say thy sweet is bitter,
When thy ripe fruit is such
    As nothing can be sweeter.
Fair house of joy and bliss,
Where truest pleasure is,
        I do adore thee.
I know thee what thou art,
I serve thee with my heart
        And fall before thee.

ANONYMOUS (*17th century*)

54 From *The Angel in the House*

An idle poet, here and there,
    Looks round him; but, for all the rest,
The world, unfathomably fair,
    Is duller than a witling's jest.
Love wakes men, once a lifetime each;
    They lift their heavy lids, and look;
And, lo, what one sweet page can teach
    They read with joy, then shut the book.
And some give thanks, and some blaspheme,
    And most forget; but, either way,
That and the child's unheeded dream
    Is all the light of all their day.

COVENTRY PATMORE

55

By our first strange and fatal interview.

JOHN DONNE (*Elegy* XVII)

56 From *The Definition of Love*

My love is of a birth as rare
As 'tis for object strange and high:
It was begotten by Despair
Upon Impossibility.

ANDREW MARVELL

57   *To Electra*

I dare not ask a kiss,
　　I dare not beg a smile,
Lest having that, or this,
　　I might grow proud the while.

No, no, the utmost share
　　Of my desire shall be
Only to kiss that air
　　That lately kissèd thee.

ROBERT HERRICK

58

Thrice toss these oaken ashes in the air,
Thrice sit thou mute in this enchanted chair,
Then thrice-three times tie up this true love's knot,
And murmur soft 'She will or she will not.'

Go, burn these poisonous weeds in yon blue fire,
These screech-owl's feathers and this prickling briar,
This cypress gathered at a dead man's grave,
That all my fears and cares an end may have.

Then come, you Fairies! dance with me a round!
Melt her hard heart with your melodious sound!
In vain are all the charms I can devise:
She hath an art to break them with her eyes.

THOMAS CAMPION

59

I wonder, by my troth, what thou and I
Did, till we lov'd? Were we not wean'd till then?
But suck'd on country pleasures, childishly?
Or snorted we in the Seven Sleepers' den?
'Twas so; but this, all pleasures fancies be;
If ever any beauty I did see,
Which I desir'd, and got, 'twas but a dream of thee.

JOHN DONNE (*The Good-Morrow*)

O my love is like a red, red rose,
 That's newly sprung in June:
O my love is like the melodie,
 That's sweetly play'd in tune.

As fair art thou, my bonnie lass,
 So deep in love am I;
And I will love thee still, my dear,
 Till a' the seas gang dry.

Till a' the seas gang dry, my dear,
 And the rocks melt wi' the sun;
And I will love thee still, my dear,
 While the sands o' life shall run.

And fare-thee-weel, my only love!
 And fare-thee-weel a while!
And I will come again, my love,
 Tho' it were ten thousand mile.

ROBERT BURNS

61

Ask me no more where Jove bestows,
When June is past, the fading rose:
For in your beauty's orient deep
These flowers as in their causes sleep.

Ask me no more whither do stray
The golden atoms of the day:
For in pure love heaven did prepare
Those powders to enrich your hair.

Ask me no more whither doth haste
The nightingale, when May is past:
For in your sweet dividing throat
She winters, and keeps warm her note.

Ask me no more where those stars 'light
That downwards fall in dead of night:
For in your eyes they sit, and there
Fixèd become as in their sphere.

Ask me no more if east or west
The Phœnix builds her spicy nest;
For unto you at last she flies,
And in your fragrant bosom dies.

THOMAS CAREW

62   *Leander*

His body was as straight as Circe's wand;
Jove might have sipt out nectar from his hand.
Even as delicious meat is to the taste,
So was his neck in touching, and surpassed
The white of Pelops' shoulder: I could tell ye,
How smooth his breast was, and how white his belly,
And whose immortal fingers did imprint
That heavenly path with many a curious dint,
That runs along his back.

CHRISTOPHER MARLOWE
(*Hero and Leander*)

63   *Faustus Sees Helen*

Was this the face that launch'd a thousand ships,
And burnt the topless towers of Ilium?—
Sweet Helen, make me immortal with a kiss.—
Her lips suck forth my soul: see where it flies!—
Come, Helen, come, give me my soul again.
Here will I dwell, for heaven is in those lips,
And all is dross that is not Helena.
I will be Paris, and for love of thee,
Instead of Troy, shall Wittenberg be sack'd;
And I will combat with weak Menelaus,
And wear thy colours on my plumèd crest:
Yea, I will wound Achilles in the heel,
And then return to Helen for a kiss.

O, thou art fairer than the evening air
Clad in the beauty of a thousand stars;
Brighter art thou than flaming Jupiter
When he appear'd to hapless Semele;
More lovely than the monarch of the sky
In wanton Arethusa's azured arms;
And none but thou shalt be my paramour!

CHRISTOPHER MARLOWE
(*Doctor Faustus*, V, 1)

64

Love not me for comely grace,
For my pleasing eye or face,
Nor for any outward part,
No, nor for a constant heart:
    For these may fail or turn to ill,
      So thou and I shall sever:
Keep, therefore, a true woman's eye,
And love me still but know not why—
    So hast thou the same reason still
      To doat upon me ever!

ANONYMOUS (*17th century*)

65

Yes, I'm in love, I feel it now
    And Celia has undone me!
And yet I'll swear I can't tell how
    The pleasing plague stole on me.

'Tis not her face that love creates,
    For there no graces revel;
'Tis not her shape, for there the Fates
    Have rather been uncivil.

'Tis not her air, for, sure in that
    There's nothing more than common;
And all her sense is only chat,
    Like any other woman.

Her voice, her touch, might give the alarm,
  'Twas both, perhaps, or neither!
In short, 'twas that provoking charm
  Of Celia all together.

WILLIAM WHITEHEAD

66

The life so short, the craft so long to learn,
Th' assay so hard, so sharp the conquering,
The dreadful joy, alway that slit so yerne:
All this mean I by Love.

GEOFFREY CHAUCER

(The Parliament of Fowls)

67

For love is Lord of truth and loyalty,
Lifting himself out of the lowly dust
On golden plumes up to the purest sky.

EDMUND SPENSER

(Hymn in Honour of Love)

68

But creeps a whisper with a traitor tongue—
Hadst never sunned beneath this maiden's glance
Another love thou hadst as madly sung,
For love is certain but the loved one chance.

LORD DE TABLEY

('My heart is vexed')

69

Bright star, would I were steadfast as thou art—
  Not in lone splendour hung aloft the night
And watching, with eternal lids apart,
  Like nature's patient, sleepless Eremite,

The moving waters at their priestlike task
  Of pure ablution round earth's human shores,
Or gazing on the new soft-fallen mask
  Of snow upon the mountains and the moors—
No—yet still steadfast, still unchangeable,
  Pillow'd upon my fair love's ripening breast,
To feel for ever its soft fall and swell,
  Awake for ever in a sweet unrest,
Still, still to hear her tender-taken breath,
And so live ever—or else swoon to death.

JOHN KEATS

70   *To His Coy Mistress*

Had we but world enough and time,
This coyness, lady, were no crime.
We would sit down, and think which way
To walk, and pass our long love's day.
Thou by the Indian Ganges' side
Should'st rubies find; I by the tide
Of Humber would complain. I would
Love you ten years before the Flood;
And you should if you please refuse
Till the conversion of the Jews.
My vegetable love should grow
Vaster than empires, and more slow.
A hundred years should go to praise
Thine eyes, and on thy forehead gaze.
Two hundred to adore each breast;
But thirty thousand to the rest.
An age at least to every part,
And the last age should show your heart.
For, lady, you deserve this state,
Nor would I love at lower rate.
  But at my back I always hear
Time's wingèd chariot hurrying near;
And yonder all before us lie
Deserts of vast eternity.
Thy beauty shall no more be found,
Nor in thy marble vault shall sound

49

My echoing song; then worms shall try
That long preserved virginity,
And your quaint honour turn to dust,
And into ashes all my lust.
The grave's a fine and private place,
But none I think do there embrace,
  Now therefore while the youthful hue
Sits on thy skin like morning dew,
And while thy willing soul transpires
At every pore with instant fires,
Now let us sport us while we may;
And now like amorous birds of prey
Rather at once our time devour
Than languish in his slow-chapped power.
Let us roll all our strength and all
Our sweetness up into one ball,
And tear our pleasures with rough strife
Through the iron gates of life.
Thus, though we cannot make our sun
Stand still, yet we will make him run.

ANDREW MARVELL

71

Ten kisses short as one, one long as twenty.

WILLIAM SHAKESPEARE

(Venus and Adonis)

72

I saw my Lady weep,
And Sorrow proud to be exalted so
In those fair eyes where all perfections keep.
    Her face was full of woe;
But such a woe (believe me) as wins more hearts
That Mirth can do with her enticing parts.

Sorrow was there made fair,
And Passion wise; Tears a delightful thing;
Silence beyond all speech, a wisdom rare:
    She made her sighs to sing,
And all things with so sweet a sadness move
As made my heart at once both grieve and love.

    O fairer than aught else
The world can show, leave off in time to grieve!
Enough, enough: your joyful look excels:
    Tears kill the heart, believe.
O strive not to be excellent in woe,
Which only breeds your beauty's overthrow.

                    ANONYMOUS (16*th century*)

73

Follow your saint, follow with accents sweet!
Haste you, sad notes, fall at her flying feet!
There, wrapt in cloud of sorrow, pity move,
And tell the ravisher of my soul I perish for her love:
But if she scorns my never-ceasing pain,
Then burst with sighing in her sight, and ne'er return
    again!

All that I sung still to her praise did tend;
Still she was first, still she my songs did end;
Yet she my love and music both doth fly,
The music that her echo is and beauty's sympathy:
Then let my notes pursue her scornful flight!
It shall suffice that they were breathed and died for
    her delight.

                    THOMAS CAMPION

74

You, madam, are the eternal humorist,
The eternal enemy of the absolute,
Giving our vagrant moods the slightest twist!
            THOMAS STEARNS ELIOT
                    (*Conversation Galante*)

Her rage was love, and its tempestuous flame,
Like lightning, showed the heaven from whence it came.

JOHN DRYDEN

(*The Maiden Queen*, *IV*, 2)

76   *Britomart*

And feignèd still her former angry mood,
Thinking to hide the depth by troubling of the flood.

EDMUND SPENSER

(*The Faery Queen*, IV, 6)

77

So, so, break off this last lamenting kiss.

JOHN DONNE (*The Expiration*)

78   *The Lost Mistress*

All's over, then: does truth sound bitter
   As one at first believes?
Hark, 'tis the sparrows' good-night twitter
   About your cottage eaves!

And the leaf-buds on the vine are woolly,
   I noticed that, to-day;
One day more bursts them open fully
   —You know the red turns grey.

To-morrow we meet the same then, dearest?
   May I take your hand in mine?
Mere friends are we,—well, friends the merest
   Keep much that I'll resign:

For each glance of that eye so bright and black,
　　Though I keep with heart's endeavour,—
Your voice, when you wish the snowdrops back,
　　Though it stay in my soul for ever!—

Yet I will but say what mere friends say,
　　Or only a thought stronger;
I will hold your hand but as long as all may,
　　Or so very little longer!

ROBERT BROWNING

79

Since there's no help, come let us kiss and part;
Nay, I have done, you get no more of me;
And I am glad, yea, glad with all my heart,
That thus so cleanly I myself can free;
Shake hands for ever, cancel all our vows,
And when we meet at any time again,
Be it not seen in either of our brows
That we one jot of former love retain.
Now at the last gasp of love's latest breath,
When, his pulse failing, passion speechless lies,
When faith is kneeling by his bed of death,
And innocence is closing up his eyes,
　　Now if thou would'st, when all have given him over,
　　From death to life thou might'st him yet recover.

MICHAEL DRAYTON

80　　　From *Curtain*

Is it so easy, then? Goodbye no more than this
Quiet disaster? And is there cause for sorrow
That in the small white murder of one kiss
Are born two ghosts, two Hamlets, two soliloquies,
Two worlds apart, to-morrow?

HELEN SPALDING

53

Come not, when I am dead,
  To drop thy foolish tears upon my grave,
To trample round my fallen head,
  And vex the unhappy dust thou wouldst not save.
There let the wind sweep and the plover cry;
          But thou, go by.

Child, if it were thine error or thy crime
  I care no longer, being all unblest:
Wed whom thou wilt, but I am sick of Time,
  And I desire to rest.
Pass on, weak heart, and leave me where I lie:
          Go by, go by.

ALFRED, LORD TENNYSON

Go on, go on, and love away!
Mine was, another's is, the day.
Go on, go on, thou false one! now
Upon his shoulder rest thy brow,
And look into his eyes, until
Thy own, to find them colder, fill.

WALTER SAVAGE LANDOR

You have oft, for these two lips,
Neglected cassia, or the natural sweets
Of the spring-violet: they are not yet much withered.

JOHN WEBSTER

(*The White Devil*, II, 1)

I dug, beneath the cypress shade,
    What well might seem an elfin's grave;
And every pledge in earth I laid,
    That erst thy false affection gave.

I pressed them down the sod beneath;
    I placed one mossy stone above;
And twined the rose's fading wreath
    Around the sepulchre of love.

Frail as thy love, the flowers were dead,
    Ere yet the evening sun was set:
But years shall see the cypress spread,
    Immutable as my regret.

THOMAS LOVE PEACOCK

85

And I shall find some girl perhaps
    And a better one than you,
With eyes as wise, but kindlier,
    And lips as soft, but true.
    And I daresay she will do.

RUPERT BROOKE (*The Chilterns*)

86   Love and Life

All my past life is mine no more;
    The flying hours are gone,
Like transitory dreams given o'er,
Whose images are kept in store
    By memory alone.

The time that is to come is not;
    How can it then be mine?
The present moment's all my lot;
And that, as fast as it is got,
    Phillis, is only thine.

Then talk not of inconstancy,
    False hearts, and broken vows;
If I by miracle can be
This live-long minute true to thee,
    'Tis all that Heaven allows.

JAMES WILMOT, EARL OF ROCHESTER

87

So, we'll go no more a roving
    So late into the night,
Though the heart be still as loving,
    And the moon be still as bright.

For the sword outwears its sheath,
    And the soul wears out the breast,
And the heart must pause to breathe,
    And love itself have rest.

Though the night was made for loving,
    And the day returns too soon,
Yet we'll go no more a roving
    By the light of the moon.

LORD BYRON

88

O love, my love! if I no more should see
Thyself, nor on the earth the shadow of thee,
    Nor image of thine eyes in any spring,—
How then should sound upon Life's darkening slope
The ground-whirl of the perished leaves of Hope,
    The wind of Death's imperishable wing?

DANTE GABRIEL ROSSETTI
(*The House of Life*)

What then was I? She slumbered with the dead.
Glory and joy and peace had come and gone.
Doth the cloud perish, when the beams are fled
Which steeped its skirts in gold? or dark, and lone,
Doth it not through the paths of night unknown,
On outspread wings of its own wind upborne
Pour rain upon the earth? the stars are shown,
When the cold moon sharpens her silver horn
Under the sea, and make the wide night not forlorn.

PERCY BYSSHE SHELLEY
(*The Revolt of Islam*, IV, 31)

90

A slumber did my spirit seal;
   I had no human fears:
She seemed a thing that could not feel
   The touch of earthly years.

No motion has she now, no force;
   She neither hears nor sees;
Roll'd round in earth's diurnal course,
   With rocks, and stones, and trees.

WILLIAM WORDSWORTH

91   *Helen of Kirconnell*

I wish I were where Helen lies,
Night and day on me she cries;
O that I were where Helen lies,
   On fair Kirconnell lea!

Curst be the heart that thought the thought,
And curst the hand that fired the shot,
When in my arms burd Helen dropt,
   And died to succour me!

O think na ye my heart was sair,
When my Love dropp'd and spak nae mair!
There did she swoon wi' meikle care,
   On fair Kirconnell lea.

As I went down the water side,
None but my foe to be my guide,
None but my foe to be my guide,
   On fair Kirconnell lea;

I lighted down my sword to draw,
I hackèd him in pieces sma',
I hackèd him in pieces sma',
   For her sake that died for me.

O Helen fair, beyond compare!
I'll mak a garland o' thy hair,
Shall bind my heart for evermair,
   Until the day I die!

O that I were where Helen lies!
Night and day on me she cries;
Out of my bed she bids me rise,
   Says, 'Haste, and come to me!'

O Helen fair! O Helen chaste!
If I were with thee, I'd be blest,
Where thou lies low and taks thy rest,
   On fair Kirconnell lea.

I wish my grave were growing green,
A winding-sheet drawn owre my e'en,
And I in Helen's arms lying,
   On fair Kirconnell lea.

I wish I were where Helen lies!
Night and day on me she cries;
And I am weary of the skies,
   For her sake that died for me.

ANONYMOUS

Must business thee from hence remove?
Oh, that's the worst disease of love:
The poor, the foul, the false, love can
Admit, but not the busied man.
He which hath business, and makes love, doth do
Such wrong, as when a married man doth woo.

JOHN DONNE (*Break of Day*)

93

False friends I have, as well as you,
  Who daily counsel me
Fame and ambition to pursue,
  And leave off loving thee.

When I the least belief bestow
  On what such fools advise,
May I be dull enough to grow
  Most miserably wise.

CHARLES SACKVILLE, EARL OF DORSET
(*Song*)

94

When, wearied with a world of woe,
  To thy safe bosom I retire,
Where love, and peace, and truth does flow,
  May I contented there expire:

Lest once more wandering from that heaven
  I fall on some base heart unblessed,
Faithless to thee, false, unforgiven,
  And lose my everlasting rest.

JOHN WILMOT, EARL OF ROCHESTER
(*'Absent from Thee'*)

95   From *The Ecstasy*

But O alas, so long, so far
  Our bodies why do we forbear?
They are ours, though they are not we, we are
  The intelligences, they the sphere. . . .
As our blood labours to beget
  Spirits, as like souls as it can,
Because such fingers need to knit
  That subtle knot, which makes us man:
So must pure lovers' souls descend
  T'affections, and to faculties,
Which sense may reach and apprehend,
  Else a great Prince in prison lies.
To our bodies turn we then, that so
  Weak men on love reveal'd may look;
Love's mysteries in souls do grow,
  But yet the body is his book.
And if some lover, such as we,
  Have heard this dialogue of one,
Let him still mark us, he shall see
  Small change, when we are to bodies gone.

JOHN DONNE

96   *Adam and Eve Before the Fall*

Two of far nobler shape erect and tall,
Godlike erect, with native honour clad
In naked majesty seemed lords of all,
And worthy seemed, for in their looks divine
The image of their glorious Maker shone. . . .
She as a veil down to the slender waist
Her unadornèd golden tresses wore
Dishevelled, but in wanton ringlets waved
As the vine curls her tendrils, which implied
Subjection, but required with gentle sway,
And by her yielded, by him best received,
Yielded with coy submission, modest pride,
And sweet reluctant amorous delay. . . .
Imparadised in one another's arms,
The happier Eden. . . .

Here love his golden shafts employs, here lights
His constant lamp, and waves his purple wings,
Reigns here and revels : not in the bought smile
Of harlots, loveless, joyless, unendeared,
Casual fruition, nor in court amours
Mixed dance, or wanton mask, or midnight ball,
Or serenade, which the starved lover sings
To his proud fair, best quitted with disdain.
These, lulled by nightingales, embracing slept,
And on their naked limbs the flowery roof
Showered roses, which the morn repaired. Sleep on,
Blest pair ; and O yet happiest if ye seek
No happier state, and know to know no more !

JOHN MILTON (*Paradise Lost*, IV)

97   *Troilus Awaits Cressida*

                    I stalk about her door,
Like a strange soul upon the Stygian banks
Staying for waftage. . . .
I am giddy ; expectation whirls me round.
The imaginary relish is so sweet
That it enchants my sense ; what will it be,
When that the watery palate tastes indeed
Love's thrice-repurèd nectar? death, I fear me ;
Swooning destruction ; or some joy too fine,
Too subtle-potent, tuned too sharp in sweetness,
For the capacity of my ruder powers.

WILLIAM SHAKESPEARE
(*Troilus and Cressida*, III, 2)

98   From *Hero and Leander*

Wherein Leander on her quivering breast
Breathless spoke something, and sighed out the rest. . . .
Love is not full of pity, as men say,
But deaf and cruel where he means to prey.

Even as a bird, which in our hands we wring,
Forth plungeth, and oft flutters with her wing,
She trembling strove; this strife of hers (like that
Which made the world) another world begat
Of unknown joy. Treason was in her thought,
And cunningly to yield herself she sought.
Seeming not won, yet won she was at length;
In such wars women use but half their strength.
Leander now, like Theban Hercules,
Entered the orchard of the Hesperides;
Whose fruit none rightly can describe but he
That pulls or shakes it from the golden tree.

CHRISTOPHER MARLOWE

99   *Lullaby*

Beloved, may your sleep be sound
That have found it where you fed.
What were all the world's alarms
To mighty Paris when he found
Sleep upon a golden bed
That first dawn in Helen's arms?

Sleep, beloved, such a sleep
As did that wild Tristram know
When, the potion's work being done,
Roe could run or doe could leap
Under oak and beechen bough,
Roe could leap or doe could run;

Such a sleep and sound as fell
Upon Eurotas' grassy bank
When the holy bird, that there
Accomplished his predestined will,
From the limbs of Leda sank
But not from her protecting care.

WILLIAM BUTLER YEATS

Dear love, for nothing less than thee
Would I have broke this happy dream;
    It was a theme
For reason, much too strong for phantasy:
Therefore thou wak'dst me wisely; yet
My dream thou brok'st not, but continued'st it,
Thou art so truth, that thoughts of thee suffice,
To make dreams truths, and fables histories;
Enter these arms, for since thou thoughtst it best
Not to dream all my dream, let's act the rest.

As lightning, or a taper's light,
Thine eyes, and not thy noise, waked me;
    Yet I thought thee
—For thou lov'st truth—an angel at first sight;
But when I saw thou saw'st my heart,
And knew'st my thoughts beyond an angel's art,
When thou knew'st what I dreamt, when thou
        knew'st when
Excess of joy would wake me, and cam'st then,
I must confess, it could not choose but be
Profane, to think thee any thing but thee.

Coming and staying show'd thee, thee,
But rising makes me doubt, that now
    Thou art not thou.
That love is weak where fear's as strong as he;
'Tis not all spirit, pure and brave,
If mixture it of fear, shame, honour have;
Perchance as torches, which must ready be,
Men light and put out, so thou deal'st with me;
Thou cam'st to kindle, go'st to come; then I
Will dream that hope again, but else would die.

JOHN DONNE

101   *Antony*

How I loved,
Witness, ye days and nights, and all ye hours
That danced away with down upon your feet.

JOHN DRYDEN (*All for Love*, II, 1)

102

When your heart was mine, my old true love,
  And your head lay on my breast,
You could make me believe by the falling of your arm
  That the sun rose up in the West!

ANONYMOUS (Folk Song)

103

Fool, thou didst not understand
The mystic language of the eye nor hand.

JOHN DONNE (Elegy VII)

104

Do not expect again a phœnix hour,
The triple-towered sky, the dove complaining,
Sudden the rain of gold and heart's first ease
Tranced under trees by the eldritch light of sundown.

By a blazed trail our joy will be returning:
One burning hour throws light a thousand ways,
And hot blood stays into familiar gestures.
The best years wait, the body's plentitude.

Consider then, my lover, this is the end
Of the lark's ascending, the hawk's unearthly hover:
Spring season is over soon and first heatwave;
Grave-browed with cloud ponders the huge horizon.

Draw up the dew. Swell with pacific violence.
Take shape in silence. Grow as the clouds grew.
Beautiful brood the cornlands, and you are heavy;
Leafy the boughs—they also hide big fruit.

CECIL DAY LEWIS

There is a mountain and a wood between us
Where the lone shepherd and late bird have seen us,
Morning and noon and even-tide repass.
Between us now the mountain and the wood
Seem standing darker than last year they stood,
And say we must not cross, alas! alas!

WALTER SAVAGE LANDOR

106

Western wind, when wilt thou blow,
   The small rain down can rain?
Christ, if my love were in my arms
   And I in my bed again!

ANONYMOUS (16th century)

107   *The Forsaken Lover Remembers the Past*

Thankèd be fortune, it hath been otherwise
   Twenty times better; but once in speciäl,
In thin array, after a pleasant guise,
   When her loose gown from her shoulders did fall,
And she me caught in her arms long and small,
And therewith all sweetly did me kiss,
   And softly said, 'Dear heart, how like you this?'

SIR THOMAS WYATT ('They Flee From Me')

108   *Troilus Parts from Cressida*

We two, that with so many thousand sighs
Did buy each other, must poorly sell ourselves
With the rude brevity and discharge of one.
Injurious Time now, with a robber's haste,
Crams his rich thievery up, he knows not how:
As many farewells as be stars in heaven,
With distinct breath and consign'd kisses to them,

. 65   G

He fumbles up into a loose adieu;
And scants us with a single famisht kiss,
Distasted with the salt of broken tears.

WILLIAM SHAKESPEARE
(*Troilus and Cressida*, IV, 4)

109   *To Marguerite*

Yes: in the sea of life enisled,
   With echoing straits between us thrown,
Dotting the shoreless watery wild,
   We mortal millions live *alone*.
The islands feel the enclasping flow,
And then their endless bounds they know.

But when the moon their hollows lights,
   And they are swept by balms of spring,
And in their glens, on starry nights,
   The nightingales divinely sing;
And lovely notes, from shore to shore,
Across the sounds and channels pour;

O then a longing like despair
   Is to their farthest caverns sent!
For surely once, they feel, we were
   Parts of a single continent.
Now round us spreads the watery plain—
O might our marges meet again!

Who order'd that their longing's fire
   Should be, as soon as kindled, cool'd?
Who renders vain their deep desire?—
   A God, a God their severance ruled;
And bade betwixt their shores to be
The unplumb'd, salt, estranging sea.

MATTHEW ARNOLD

> I have spent
> Many a silent night in sighs and groans;
> Ran over all my thoughts, despised my fate,
> Reasoned against the reasons of my love.
> JOHN FORD (*'Tis Pity She's a Whore*, I, 3)

111   From *Eloïsa to Abelard*

Of all affliction taught a lover yet,
'Tis sure the hardest science to forget!
How shall I lose the sin, yet keep the sense,
And love the offender, yet detest the offence?
How the dear object from the crime remove,
Or how distinguish penitence from love?
Unequal task! a passion to resign,
For hearts so touch'd, so pierc'd, so lost as mine.
Ere such a soul regains its peaceful state,
How often must it love, how often hate!
How often hope, despair, resent, regret,
Conceal, disdain—do all things but forget.

ALEXANDER POPE

112   *Renouncement*

I must not think of thee; and, tired yet strong,
    I shun the love that lurks in all delight—
    The love of thee—and in the blue heaven's height,
And in the dearest passage of a song.
Oh, just beyond the fairest thoughts that throng
    This breast, the thought of thee waits hidden yet
    bright;
    But it must never, never come in sight;
I must stop short of thee the whole day long.
But when sleep comes to close each difficult day,
    And night gives pause to the long watch I keep,
    And all my bonds I needs must loose apart,
Must doff my will as raiment laid away,—
    With the first dream that comes with the first sleep
    I run, I run, I am gather'd to thy heart.

ALICE MEYNELL

Leave me, O Love, which reachest but to dust,
And thou, my mind, aspire to higher things!
Grow rich in that which never taketh rust:
Whatever fades, but fading pleasure brings.
Draw in thy beams, and humble all thy might
To that sweet yoke where lasting freedoms be;
Which breaks the clouds and opens forth the light
That doth both shine and give us sight to see.
O take fast hold! let that light be thy guide
In this small course which birth draws out to death,
And think how evil becometh him to slide
Who seeketh Heaven, and comes of heavenly breath.
     Then farewell, world! thy uttermost I see:
     Eternal Love, maintain thy life in me!

SIR PHILIP SIDNEY

The expense of spirit in a waste of shame
Is lust in action; and till action, lust
Is perjured, murderous, bloody, full of blame,
Savage, extreme, rude, cruel, not to trust;
Enjoy'd no sooner but despisèd straight;
Past reason hunted; and, no sooner had,
Past reason hated, as a swallow'd bait
On purpose laid to make the taker mad:
Mad in pursuit, and in possession so;
Had, having, and in quest to have, extreme;
A bliss in proof, and proved, a very woe;
Before, a joy proposed; behind, a dream.
  All this the world well knows; yet none knows
    well
  To shun the heaven that leads men to this hell.

WILLIAM SHAKESPEARE

Mark where the pressing wind shoots javelin-like
Its skeleton shadow on the broad-back'd wave!
Here is a fitting spot to dig Love's grave;
Here where the ponderous breakers plunge and strike,
And dart their hissing tongues high up the sand:
In hearing of the ocean, and in sight
Of those ribb'd wind-streaks running into white.
If I the death of Love had deeply plann'd,
I never could have made it half so sure,
As by the unblest kisses which upbraid
The full-waked sense; or failing that, degrade!
'Tis morning: but no morning can restore
What we have forfeited. I see no sin:
The wrong is mixed. In tragic life, God wot,
No villain need be! Passions spin the plot:
We are betrayed by what is false within.

GEORGE MEREDITH (*Modern Love*)

116   *Frankford Forgives His Dying Wife*

Even as I hope for pardon at that day
When the great Judge of heaven in scarlet sits,
So be thou pardoned. Though thy rash offence
Divorced our bodies, thy repentant tears
Unite our souls.

THOMAS HEYWOOD
(*A Woman Killed with Kindness*, *V*, 6)

117   *Eve Prepares to Leave Paradise with Adam*

Wearied I fell asleep: but now lead on;
In me is no delay; with thee to go,
Is to stay here; without thee here to stay,
Is to go hence unwilling; thou to me
Art all things under Heaven, all places thou,
Who for my wilful crime art banished hence.

JOHN MILTON (*Paradise Lost*, XII)

Let me not to the marriage of true minds
Admit impediments. Love is not love
Which alters when it alteration finds,
Or bends with the remover to remove:
O, no! it is an ever-fixèd mark,
That looks on tempests and is never shaken;
It is the star to every wandering bark,
Whose worth's unknown, although his height be taken.
Love's not Time's fool, though rosy lips and cheeks
Within his bending sickle's compass come;
Love alters not with his brief hours and weeks,
But bears it out even to the edge of doom,
    If this be error, and upon me proved,
    I never writ, nor no man ever loved.

WILLIAM SHAKESPEARE

119   *To Celia*

Not, Celia, that I juster am
    Or better than the rest!
For I would change each hour, like them,
    Were not my heart at rest.

But I am tied to very thee
    By every thought I have;
Thy face I only care to see,
    Thy heart I only crave.

All that in woman is adored
    In thy dear self I find—
For the whole sex can but afford
    The handsome and the kind.

Why then should I seek further store,
    And still make love anew?
When change itself can give no more,
    'Tis easy to be true!

SIR CHARLES SEDLEY

I vowed unvarying faith, and she,
  To whom in full I pay that vow,
Rewards me with variety
  Which men who change can never know.

COVENTRY PATMORE

(*The Angel in the House*)

121   *The Apparition*

My dead love came to me, and said:
  'God gives me one hour's rest
To spend upon the earth with thee:
  How shall we spend it best?'

'Why, as of old,' I said, and so
  We quarrelled as of old.
But when I turned to make my peace
  That one short hour was told.

STEPHEN PHILLIPS

122   *Remembrance*

Cold in the earth—and the deep snow piled above thee,
Far, far removed, cold in the dreary grave!
Have I forgot, my only Love, to love thee,
Severed at last by Time's all-severing wave?

Now, when alone, do my thoughts no longer hover
Over the mountains, on that northern shore,
Resting their wings where heath and fern-leaves cover
Thy noble heart for ever, ever more?

Cold in the earth—and fifteen wild Decembers
From those brown hills have melted into spring:
Faithful, indeed, is the spirit that remembers
After such years of change and suffering!

Sweet Love of youth, forgive, if I forget thee,
While the world's tide is bearing me along;
Other desires and other hopes beset me,
Hopes which obscure, but cannot do thee wrong!

No later light has lightened up my heaven,
No second morn has ever shone for me;
All my life's bliss from thy dear life was given,
All my life's bliss is in the grave with thee.

But, when the days of golden dreams had perished,
And even Despair was powerless to destroy,
Then did I learn how existence could be cherished,
Strengthened, and fed without the aid of joy.

Then did I check the tears of useless passion—
Weaned my young soul from yearning after thine;
Sternly denied its burning wish to hasten
Down to that tomb already more than mine.

And, even yet, I dare not let it languish,
Dare not indulge in memory's rapturous pain;
Once drinking deep of that divinest anguish,
How could I seek the empty world again?

EMILY JANE BRONTË

123   From *The Relique*

When my grave is broke up again
   Some second guest to entertain,
(For graves have learn'd that woman-head
To be to more than one a bed)
   And he that digs it, spies
A bracelet of bright hair about the bone,
   Will he not let us alone,
And think that there a loving couple lies,
Who thought that this device might be some way
To make their souls, at the last busy day,
Meet at this grave, and make a little stay?

JOHN DONNE

Anna.: Be not deceived . . .
          This banquet is an harbinger of death
          To you and me; resolve yourself it is,
          And be prepared to welcome it.
Gio.:   Well, then;
          The schoolmen teach that all this globe of earth
          Shall be consumed to ashes in a minute.
Anna.: So I have read too.
Gio.:   But 'twere somewhat strange
          To see the waters burn: could I believe
          This might be true, I could believe as well
          There might be hell or Heaven.
Anna.:   That's most certain.
Gio.:   A dream, a dream! else in this other world
          We should know one another.
Anna.:   So we shall.
Gio.:   Have you heard so?
Anna.:   For certain.
Gio.:   But d'ye think
          That I shall see you there?—You look on me.—
          May we kiss one another, prate or laugh,
          Or do as we do here?
Anna.:   I know not that.

                        JOHN FORD
                  ('*Tis Pity She's a Whore*, V, 5)

125   From *Exequy on His Wife*

            Sleep on, my Love, in thy cold bed
            Never to be disquieted!
            My last good-night! Thou wilt not wake
            Till I thy fate shall overtake:
            Till age, or grief, or sickness must
            Marry my body to that dust
            It so much loves; and fill the room
            My heart keeps empty in thy tomb.
            Stay for me there: I will not fail
            To meet thee in that hollow vale.

                        73

And think not much of my delay:
I am already on the way,
And follow thee with all the speed
Desire can make, or sorrows breed.
Each minute is a short degree
And every hour a step towards thee. . . .
But hark! my pulse, like a soft drum,
Beats my approach, tells thee I come;
And slow howe'er my marches be
I shall at last sit down by thee.

HENRY KING

126

I am dying, Egypt, dying; only
I here importune death awhile, until
Of many thousand kisses the poor last
I lay upon thy lips.

WILLIAM SHAKESPEARE
(Antony and Cleopatra, IV, 13)

127

Now with his love, now in his coldë grave,
Alone, withouten any company.

GEOFFREY CHAUCER (The Knight's Tale)

3

ART

The section begins with poetry on buildings and architecture, and continues with poetry on sculpture and other plastic arts, painting, music, drama, dress, and ornament. From 162 onwards, poets speak or sing about their own art, including (162–165) its practice by others whom they decline to admire.

128   *Petra*

Match me such marvel save in Eastern clime,
A rose-red city half as old as time.
                    JOHN WILLIAM BURGON (*Petra*)

129 *On a Winged Bull in the British Museum,*
              Excavated at Nineveh

What vows, what rites, what prayers preferr'd,
What songs has the strange image heard?
In what blind vigil stood interr'd
For ages, till an English word
    Broke silence first at Nineveh?

Oh when upon each sculptured court,
Where even the wind might not resort,—
O'er which Time passed, of like import
With the wild Arab boys at sport,—
    A living face looked in to see:—
Oh seemed it not—the spell once broke—
As though the carven warriors woke,
As though the shaft the string forsook,
The cymbals clashed, the chariots shook,
    And there was life in Nineveh?
                    DANTE GABRIEL ROSSETTI
                         (*The Burden of Nineveh*)

To save the Athenian walls from ruin bare.

JOHN MILTON (*Sonnet*)

131

See the wild waste of all-devouring years!
How Rome her own sad sepulchre appears,
With nodding arches, broken temples spread!
The very tombs now vanished like their dead!

ALEXANDER POPE (*Epistle to Mr. Addison*)

132   *The Grave of Keats*

Or go to Rome, which is the sepulchre,
Oh, not of him, but of our joy; 'tis nought
That ages, empires, and religions there
Lie buried in the ravage they have wrought;
For such as he can lend,—they borrow not
Glory from those who made the world their prey;
And he is gathered to the kings of thought
Who waged contention with their time's decay,
And of the past are all that cannot pass away.

Go thou to Rome,—at once the Paradise,
The grave, the city, and the wilderness;
And where its wrecks like shattered mountains rise
And flowering weeds and fragrant copses dress
The bones of Desolation's nakedness
Pass, till the Spirit of the spot shall lead
Thy footsteps to a slope of green access
Where, like an infant's smile, over the dead,
A light of laughing flowers along the grass is spread.

And grey walls moulder round, on which dull Time
Feeds, like slow fire upon a hoary brand,
And one keen pyramid with wedge sublime,
Pavilioning the dust of him who planned
This refuge for his memory, doth stand
Like flame transformed to marble. . . .

PERCY BYSSHE SHELLEY (*Adonais*)

Bitter, bitter, oh! to behold
  The grass to grow
Where the walls of Walsingham
  So stately did show.
Such were the works of Walsingham
  While she did stand!
Such are the wracks as now do show
  Of that holy land!
Level, level, with the ground
  The towers do lie,
Which with their golden glittering tops
  Pierced once to the sky! . . .

          ANONYMOUS (*16th century*)

134   *King's College Chapel, Cambridge*

Tax not the royal Saint with vain expense,
With ill-matched aims the Architect who planned—
Albeit labouring for a scanty band
Of white-robed Scholars only—this immense
And glorious Work of fine intelligence!
Give all thou canst; high Heaven rejects the lore
Of nicely-calculated less or more;
So deemed the man who fashioned for the sense
These lofty pillars, spread that branching roof
Self-poised, and scooped into ten thousand cells,
Where light and shade repose, where music dwells
Lingering—and wandering on as loth to die;
Like thoughts whose very sweetness yieldeth proof
That they were born for immortality.

          WILLIAM WORDSWORTH

135   *On the Burial of Addison in Westminster*
                  Abbey

Can I forget the dismal light that gave
My soul's best part for ever to the grave!
How silent did his old companions tread
By midnight lamps the mansions of the dead,

Through breathing statues, then unheeded things,
Through rows of warriors, and through walks of
    kings!
What awe did the slow solemn knell inspire;
The pealing organ, and the pausing choir;
The duties by the lawn-robed prelate paid;
And the last words, that dust to dust conveyed!

THOMAS TICKELL

(*To the Earl of Warwick on the Death of Mr. Addison*)

136

Where longs to fall that rifted spire,
    As weary of th' insulting air;
The poet's thought, the warrior's fire,
    The lover's sighs are sleeping there.

JOHN LANGHORNE (*The Wall-Flower*)

137   *The Temple of Venus at Sestos*

So fair a church as this, had Venus none;
The walls were of discoloured jasper stone,
Wherein was Proteus carvèd, and o'erhead
A lively vine of green sea-agate spread;
Where by one hand, light-headed Bacchus hung,
And with the other, wine from grapes outwrung.
Of crystal shining fair the pavement was;
The town of Sestos call'd it Venus' glass.
There might you see the gods in sundry shapes,
Committing heady riots, incest, rapes.

CHRISTOPHER MARLOWE

(*Hero and Leander*)

138

Praxitelean shapes, whose marble smiles
Fill the hushed air with everlasting love.

PERCY BYSSHE SHELLEY

(*Prometheus Unbound*, III, 3)

From *Ode on a Grecian Urn*

Heard melodies are sweet, but those unheard
   Are sweeter; therefore, ye soft pipes, play on;
Not to the sensual ear, but, more endear'd,
   Pipe to the spirit ditties of no tone:
Fair youth, beneath the trees, thou canst not leave
   Thy song, nor ever can those trees be bare;
     Bold Lover, never, never canst thou kiss,
Though winning near the goal—yet, do not grieve;
     She cannot fade, though thou hast not thy bliss,
   For ever wilt thou love, and she be fair!

Ah, happy, happy boughs! that cannot shed
   Your leaves, nor ever bid the Spring adieu;
And, happy melodist, unwearièd,
   For ever piping songs for ever new;
More happy love! more happy, happy love!
   For ever warm and still to be enjoy'd,
     For ever panting and for ever young;
All breathing human passion far above,
     That leaves a heart high-sorrowful and cloy'd,
     A burning forehead, and a parching tongue.

JOHN KEATS

From *Sailing to Byzantium*

Once out of nature I shall never take
My bodily form from any natural thing,
But such a form as Grecian goldsmiths make
Of hammered gold and gold enamelling
To keep a drowsy emperor awake;
Or set upon a golden bough to sing
To lords and ladies of Byzantium
Of what is past, or passing, or to come.

WILLIAM BUTLER YEATS

I shall keep your honour safe;
With mine I trust you, as the sculptor trusts
Yon marble woman with the marble rose,
Loose on her hand, she never will let fall,
In graceful, slight, silent security.

ROBERT BROWNING
(*Colombe's Birthday*, V)

142 The Bronze Colossus in the City of Dreadful Night

(*After Dürer's 'Melancholia'*)

Low-seated she leans forward massively,
  With cheek on clenched left hand, the forearm's might
Erect, its elbow on her rounded knee;
  Across a clasped book in her lap the right
Upholds a pair of compasses; she gazes
With full set eyes, but wandering in thick mazes
  Of sombre thought beholds no outward sight. . . .

But as if blacker night could dawn on night,
  With tenfold gloom on moonless night unstarred,
A sense more tragic than defeat and blight,
  More desperate than strife with hope debarred,
More fatal than the adamantine Never
Encompassing her passionate endeavour,
  Dawns glooming in her tenebrous regard:

The sense that every struggle brings defeat
  Because Fate holds no prize to crown success;
That all the oracles are dumb or cheat
  Because they have no secret to express;
That none can pierce the vast black veil uncertain
Because there is no light beyond the curtain;
  That all is vanity and nothingness.

Titanic from her high throne in the north,
    That City's sombre Patroness and Queen,
In bronze sublimity she gazes forth
    Over her Capital of teen and threne,
Over the river with its isles and bridges,
The marsh and moorland, to the stern rock-ridges,
    Confronting them with a coëval mien.

The moving moon and stars from east to west
    Circle before her in the sea of air;
Shadows and gleams glide round her solemn rest.
    Her subjects often gaze up to her there:
The strong to drink new strength of iron endurance,
The weak new terrors; all, renewed assurance
    And confirmation of the old despair.

JAMES THOMSON (*The City of Dreadful Night*)

143

With hue like that when some great painter dips
His pencil in the gloom of earthquake and eclipse.

PERCY BYSSHE SHELLEY
(*The Revolt of Islam*, V, 23)

144   From *The Portrait*

In painting her I shrined her face
    Mid mystic trees, where light falls in
Hardly at all; a covert place
    Where you might think to find a din
Of doubtful talk, and a live flame
Wandering, and many a shape whose name
    Not itself knoweth, and old dew,
    And your own footsteps meeting you,
And all things going as they came.

DANTE GABRIEL ROSSETTI

You have a full wind, and a false heart, Theseus! . . .
                              Could the gods know this,
And not, of all their number, raise a storm?
But they are all as evil. This false smile
Was well express'd; just such another caught me. . . .
Fie, you have miss'd it here, Antiphila,
You are much mistaken, wench:
These colours are not dull and pale enough
To show a soul so full of misery
As this sad lady's was. Do it by me;
Do it again by me, the lost Aspatia,
And you shall find all true but the wild island.
Suppose I stand upon the sea-beach now,
Mine arms thus, and mine hair blown with the wind,
Wild as that desert; and let all about me
Be teachers of my story. Do my face
(If thou hadst ever feeling of a sorrow)
Thus, thus, Antiphila; strive to make me look
Like Sorrow's monument; and the trees about me,
Let them be dry and leafless; let the rocks
Groan with continual surges, and behind me
Make all a desolation. Look, look, wenches,
A miserable life of this poor picture! . . .
Upon that point fix all our eyes, that point there;
Make a dull silence, till you feel a sudden sadness
Give us new souls.

FRANCIS BEAUMONT and JOHN FLETCHER
(*The Maid's Tragedy*, *II*, 2)

146   *The Bower of Bliss*

Eftsoones they heard a most melodious sound
Of all that mote delight a dainty ear,
Such as at once might not on living ground,
Save in this paradise, be heard elsewhere:

Right hard it was for wight which did it hear
To read what manner music that mote be;
For all that pleasing is to living ear
Was there consorted in one harmony;
Birds, voices, instruments, winds, waters, all agree:

The joyous birds, shrouded in cheerful shade,
Their notes unto the voice attempered sweet;
The angelical soft trembling voices made
To th' instruments divine respondence meet;
The silver-sounding instruments did meet
With the base murmur of the waters' fall;
The waters' fall with difference discreet,
Now soft, now loud, unto the wind did call;
The gentle warbling wind low answerèd to all.

EDMUND SPENSER
(*The Faery Queen*, II, 12)

147   *The Song of the Angelic Troop*

Sometimes a-dropping from the sky
I heard the skylark sing;
Sometimes all little birds that are,
How they seemed to fill the sea and air
With their sweet jargoning!

And now 'twas like all instruments,
Now like a lonely flute;
And now it is an angel's song,
That makes the Heavens be mute.

It ceased; yet still the sails made on
A pleasant noise till noon,
A noise like of a hidden brook
In the leafy month of June,
That to the sleeping woods all night
Singeth a quiet tune.

SAMUEL TAYLOR COLERIDGE
(*The Ancient Mariner*)

148   *God the Father Returns to Heaven after*
the Creation

                    Up he rode
Followed with acclamation and the sound
Symphonious of ten thousand harps that tuned
Angelic harmonies: the earth, the air
Resounded, (thou remember'st for thou heardst)
The heavens and all the constellations rung,
The planets in their stations listening stood,
While the bright pomp ascended jubilant.
                 JOHN MILTON (*Paradise Lost*, VII)

149   *Nuns*

Chanting faint hymns to the cold, fruitless moon.
            WILLIAM SHAKESPEARE
            (*A Midsummer Night's Dream*, I, 1)

150   *Adam and Eve in Paradise*

               How often from the steep
Of echoing hill or thicket have we heard
Celestial voices to the midnight air.
           JOHN MILTON (*Paradise Lost*, IV)

151

The silver snarling trumpets 'gan to chide.
          JOHN KEATS (*The Eve of St. Agnes*)

152   *A Duel between a Nightingale and a*
Lute-Player

                 For every several strain
The well-shaped youth could touch, she sung her own;
He could not run division with more art
Upon his quaking instrument than she,
The nightingale, did with her various notes
Reply to . . .

Some time thus spent, the young man grew at last
Into a pretty anger, that a bird,
Whom art had never taught cliffs, moods, or notes,
Should vie with him for mastery, whose study
Had busied many hours to perfect practice:
To end the controversy, in a rapture
Upon his instrument he plays so swiftly,
So many voluntaries and so quick,
That there was curiosity and cunning,
Concord in discord, lines of differing method
Meeting in one full centre of delight.

JOHN FORD (*The Lover's Melancholy*, I, 1)

153   *Upon a Company of Bad Dancers to*
Good Music

How ill the motion to the music suits!
So Orpheus fiddled, and so danced the brutes.

GEORGE JEFFREYS

154   *On David Garrick*

On the stage he was natural, simple, affecting;
'Twas only that when he was off he was acting.

OLIVER GOLDSMITH (*Retaliation*)

155

'Tis better in a play
Be Agamemnon, than himself indeed.
How oft, with danger of the field beset,
Or with home-mutinies, would he un-be
Himself; or, over cruel altars weeping,
Wish, that with putting off a vizard he
Might his true inward sorrow lay aside!
The shows of things are better than themselves.
How doth it stir this airy part of us
To hear our poets tell imagined fights
And the strange blows that feignèd courage gives!

When I Achilles hear upon the stage
Speak honour and the greatness of his soul,
Methinks I too could on a Phrygian spear
Run boldly, and make tales for after times:
But when we come to act it in the deed,
Death mars this bravery, and the ugly fears
Of the other world sit on the proudest brow;
And boasting valour loseth his red cheek.

ANONYMOUS (17th century) (*The Tragedy of Nero*, III, 3)

156   *Delight in Disorder*

A sweet disorder in the dress
Kindles in clothes a wantonness:
A lawn about the shoulders thrown
Into a fine distraction;
An erring lace, which here and there
Enthralls the crimson stomacher;
A cuff neglectful, and thereby
Ribands to flow confusedly;
A winning wave, deserving note,
In the tempestuous petticoat;
A careless shoe-string, in whose tie
I see a wild civility,—
Do more bewitch me, than when art
Is too precise in every part.

ROBERT HERRICK

157   From *The Rape of the Lock*

And now, unveil'd, the toilet stands display'd,
Each silver vase in mystic order laid.
First, rob'd in white, the nymph intent adores,
With head uncover'd, the cosmetic pow'rs.
A heav'nly image in the glass appears;
To that she bends, to that her eyes she rears;
Th' inferior Priestess, at her altar's side,
Trembling begins the sacred rites of Pride.
Unnumber'd treasures ope at once, and here
The various off'rings of the world appear;

From each she nicely culls with curious toil,
And decks the goddess with the glitt'ring spoil.
This casket India's glowing gems unlocks,
And all Arabia breathes from yonder box.
The tortoise here and elephant unite,
Transform'd to combs, the speckled, and the white.
Here files of pins extend their shining rows,
Puffs, powders, patches, Bibles, billet-doux.
Now awful Beauty puts on all its arms;
The fair each moment rises in her charms,
Repairs her smiles, awakens ev'ry grace,
And calls forth all the wonders of her face.

ALEXANDER POPE

158   *Antony's First Meeting with Cleopatra*

The barge she sat in, like a burnish'd throne,
Burn'd on the water; the poop was beaten gold;
Purple the sails, and so perfumed that
The winds were love-sick with them; the oars were
    silver,
Which to the tune of flutes kept stroke, and made
The water which they beat to follow faster,
As amorous of their strokes. For her own person,
It beggar'd all description; she did lie
In her pavilion—cloth-of-gold of tissue—
O'er-picturing that Venus where we see
The fancy outwork nature; on each side her
Stood pretty dimpled boys, like smiling Cupids,
With divers-colour'd fans, whose wind did seem
To glow the delicate cheeks which they did cool,
And what they undid did . . .
Her gentlewoman, like the Nereides,
So many mermaids, tended her i' the eyes,
And made their bends adornings; at the helm
A seeming mermaid steers; the silken tackle
Swell with the touches of those flower-soft hands,
That yarely frame the office.

WILLIAM SHAKESPEARE
(*Antony and Cleopatra*, I, 2)

When she came in like starlight, hid with jewels.

BEN JONSON (*Volpone*, III, 7)

160

The diamond there attracts the wondrous sight,
Proud of its thousand dyes, and luxury of light.

THOMAS GRAY (after TASSO)

161　　　　From *The Last Ride Together*

Fail I alone, in words and deeds?
Why, all men strive and who succeeds?
We rode; it seemed my spirit flew,
Saw other regions, cities new,
　　As the world rushed by on either side.
I thought,—All labour, yet no less
Bear up beneath their unsuccess.
Look at the end of work, contrast
The petty Done, the Undone vast,
This Present of theirs with the hopeful Past!
　　I hoped she would love me: here we ride.

What hand and brain went ever paired?
What heart alike conceived and dared?
What act proved all its thought had been?
What will but felt the fleshly screen?
　　We ride and I see her bosom heave.
There's many a crown for who can reach.
Ten lines, a statesman's life in each!
The flag stuck on a heap of bones,
A soldier's doing! what atones?
They scratch his name on the Abbey-stones.
　　My riding is better, by their leave.

88

What does it all mean, poet? Well,
Your brain's beat into rhythm—you tell
What we felt only; you expressed
You hold things beautiful the best,
   And pace them in rhyme so, side by side.
'Tis something, nay 'tis much—but then,
Have you yourself what's best for men?
Are you—poor, sick, old ere your time—
Nearer one whit your own sublime
Than we who never have turned a rhyme?
   Sing, riding's a joy! For me, I ride.

And you, great sculptor—so, you gave
A score of years to Art, her slave,
And that's your Venus—whence we turn
To yonder girl that fords the burn!
   You acquiesce, and shall I repine?
What, man of music, you grown gray
With notes and nothing else to say,
Is this your sole praise from a friend?—
'Greatly his opera's strains intend,
But in music we know how fashions end!'
   I gave my youth—but we ride, in fine.

ROBERT BROWNING

162   *On Peter Robinson*

Here lies the preacher, judge, and poet, Peter,
Who broke the laws of God, and man, and metre.

LORD JEFFREY

163   *On Elkanah Settle*

His Poetry

Doeg, though without knowing how or why,
Made still a blundering kind of melody;
Spurred boldly on, and dashed through thick and thin,
Through sense and nonsense, never out nor in;

Free from all meaning, whether good or bad,
And in one word, heroically mad.
He was too warm on picking-work to dwell,
But faggoted his notions as they fell,
And, if they rhymed and rattled, all was well.

JOHN DRYDEN

(*Absalom and Achitophel*)

His Poem on the Lord Mayor's Procession

Now night descending, the proud scene was o'er,
But lived in Settle's numbers one day more.

ALEXANDER POPE (*The Dunciad*)

164 *On Thomas Shadwell*

Now stop your noses, readers, all and some,
For here's a tun of midnight work to come,
Og from a treason-tavern rolling home,
Round as a globe, and liquored every chink,
Goodly and great he sails behind his link.
With all this bulk there's nothing lost in Og,
For every inch that is not fool is rogue . . .
When wine has given him courage to blaspheme,
He curses God, but God before cursed him . . .
But though Heaven made him poor (with reverence
   speaking)
He never was a poet of God's making;
The midwife laid her hand on his thick skull
With this prophetic blessing—*Be thou dull*;
Drink, swear, and roar, forbear no lewd delight
Fit for thy bulk, do anything but write. . . .
Eat opium, mingle arsenic in thy drink,
Still thou mayst live, avoiding pen and ink.
I see, I see, 'tis counsel given in vain,
For treason botched in rhyme will be thy bane . . .
Doeg, whom God for mankind's mirth has made,
O'ertops thy talent in thy very trade;
Doeg to thee, thy paintings are so coarse,
A poet is, though he's the poet's horse.

A double noose thou on thy neck dost pull
For writing treason and for writing dull;
To die for faction is a common evil,
But to be hanged for nonsense is the devil. . . .
I will not rake the dunghill of thy crimes,
For who would read thy life that reads thy rhymes?

JOHN DRYDEN
(*Absalom and Achitophel*)

165 *To ——*

Forget not, brother singer! that though Prose
   Can never be too truthful or too wise,
Song is not Truth, not Wisdom, but the rose
   Upon Truth's lips, the light in Wisdom's eyes.

SIR WILLIAM WATSON

166 *Ode to Maia*

Mother of Hermes! and still youthful Maia!
      May I sing to thee
As thou wast hymnèd on the shores of Baiae?
      Or may I woo thee
In earlier Sicilian? or thy smiles
Seek as they once were sought, in Grecian isles,
By bards who died content on pleasant sward,
Leaving great verse unto a little clan?
O, give me their old vigour, and unheard
Save of the quiet primrose, and the span
      Of heaven, and few ears,
Rounded by thee, my song should die away
      Content as theirs,
Rich in the simple worship of a day.

JOHN KEATS

167

Or on blind Homer's heart a wingèd thought.

PERCY BYSSHE SHELLEY
(*The Witch of Atlas*)

Loving in truth, and fain my love in verse to show,
That the dear She might take some pleasure of my pain,
Pleasure might cause her read, reading might make her
    know,
Knowledge might pity win, and pity grace obtain,
  I sought fit words to paint the blackest face of woe,
Studying inventions fine, her wits to entertain,
Oft turning others' leaves to see if thence would flow
Some fresh and fruitful shower upon my sunburnt brain.
  But words came halting out, wanting Invention's stay;
Invention, Nature's child, fled stepdame Study's blows;
And others' feet still seem'd but strangers in my way;
Thus great with child to speak, and helpless in my throes,
  Biting my tongue and pen, beating myself for spite,
'Fool,' said my Muse to me, 'look in thy heart and write.'

SIR PHILIP SIDNEY

169   *A Prayer for Old Age*

God guard me from those thoughts men think
In the mind alone;
He that sings a lasting song
Thinks in a marrow-bone;

From all that makes a wise old man
That can be praised of all;
O what am I that I should not seem
For the song's sake a fool?

I pray—for fashion's word is out
And prayer comes round again—
That I may seem, though I die old,
A foolish, passionate man.

WILLIAM BUTLER YEATS

I know the ways of Pleasure, the sweet strains,
　The lullings and the relishes of it;
The propositions of hot blood and brains;
　What mirth and music mean; what love and wit
Have done these twenty hundred years and more;
I know the projects of unbridled store:
My stuff is flesh, not brass; my senses live. . . .

GEORGE HERBERT (*The Pearl*)

171　From *The Prelude*

Magnificent

The morning rose, in memorable pomp,
Glorious as e'er I had beheld—in front,
The sea lay laughing at a distance; near,
The solid mountains shone, bright as the clouds,
Grain-tinctured, drenched in empyrean light;
And in the meadows and the lower grounds
Was all the sweetness of a common dawn—
Dews, vapours, and the melody of birds,
And labourers going forth to till the fields.
Ah! need I say, dear Friend! that to the brim
My heart was full; I made no vows, but vows
Were then made for me; bond unknown to me
Was given, that I should be, else sinning greatly,
A dedicated Spirit.

WILLIAM WORDSWORTH

172

Why did I write? what sin to me unknown
Dipt me in ink, my parents', or my own?
As yet a child, not yet a fool to fame,
I lisp'd in numbers, for the numbers came.
I left no calling for this idle trade,
No duty broke, no father disobey'd.
The Muse but serv'd to ease some friend, not wife,
To help me thro' this long disease, my life.

ALEXANDER POPE
(*Epistle to Dr. Arbuthnot*)

          Most wretched men
Are cradled into poetry by wrong:
They learn in suffering what they teach in song.

                    PERCY BYSSHE SHELLEY
                          (*Julian and Maddalo*)

174   *A Musical Instrument*

What was he doing, the great god Pan,
    Down in the reeds by the river?
Spreading ruin and scattering ban,
Splashing and paddling with hoofs of a goat,
And breaking the golden lilies afloat
    With the dragon-fly on the river.

He tore out a reed, the great god Pan,
    From the deep cool bed of the river;
The limpid water turbidly ran,
And the broken lilies a-dying lay,
And the dragon-fly had fled away,
    Ere he brought it out of the river.

High on the shore sat the great god Pan,
    While turbidly flowed the river;
And hacked and hewed as a great god can
With his hard bleak steel at the patient reed,
Till there was not a sign of the leaf indeed
    To prove it fresh from the river.

He cut it short, did the great god Pan
    (How tall it stood in the river!),
Then drew the pith, like the heart of a man,
Steadily from the outside ring,
And notched the poor dry empty thing
    In holes, as he sat by the river.

'This is the way,' laughed the great god Pan
    (Laughed while he sat by the river),
'The only way, since gods began
To make sweet music, they could succeed.'
Then dropping his mouth to a hole in the reed,
    He blew in power by the river.

Sweet, sweet, sweet, O Pan!
    Piercing sweet by the river!
Blinding sweet, O great god Pan!
The sun on the hill forgot to die,
And the lilies revived, and the dragon-fly
    Came back to dream on the river.

Yet half a beast is the great god Pan,
    To laugh as he sits by the river,
Making a poet out of a man:
The true gods sigh for the cost and pain—
For the reed which grows nevermore again
    As a reed with the reeds of the river.
                ELIZABETH BARRETT BROWNING

175   From *The Flower*

And now in age I bud again,
After so many deaths I live and write;
    I once more smell the dew and rain,
And relish versing: O my only light,
            It cannot be
            That I am he
On whom Thy tempests fell all night.
                GEORGE HERBERT

176   *Burns on His Own Poetry*

From   *To James Smith*

Some rhyme a neebor's name to lash;
Some rhyme (vain thought!) for needfu' cash;
Some rhyme to court the country clash,
    An' raise a din;
For me, an aim I never fash;
    I rhyme for fun. . . .

95

O ye douce folk, that live by rule,
Grave, tideless-blooded, calm and cool,
Compared wi' you—O fool! fool! fool!
    How much unlike!
Your hearts are just a standing pool,
    Your lives, a dyke!

From   *Epistle to J. Lapraik*

Give me ae spark o' Nature's fire,
That's a' the learning I desire;
Then tho' I drudge thro' dub an' mire
    At pleugh or cart,
My Muse, though hamely in attire,
    May touch the heart.

ROBERT BURNS

177

My whole life I have lived in pleasant thought,
As if life's business were a summer mood;
As if all needful things would come unsought
To genial faith, still rich in genial good;
But how can He expect that others should
Build for him, sow for him, and at his call
Love him, who for himself will take no heed at all?

I thought of Chatterton, the marvellous Boy,
The sleepless Soul that perished in his pride;
Of Him who walked in glory and in joy
Following his plough, along the mountain-side:
By our own spirits are we deified:
We Poets in our youth begin in gladness;
But thereof come in the end despondency and madness. . . .

My former thoughts returned: the fear that kills;
And hope that is unwilling to be fed;
Cold, pain, and labour, and all fleshly ills;
And mighty Poets in their misery dead.

WILLIAM WORDSWORTH
(*Resolution and Independence*)

Seven wealthy towns contend for Homer dead
Through which the living Homer begged his bread.
THOMAS SEWARD, after JOHN HEYWOOD

179 ## From *Shakespeare*

And thou, who didst the stars and sunbeams know,
Self-school'd, self-scann'd, self-honour'd, self-secure,
Didst walk on earth unguess'd at. Better so!
All pains the immortal spirit must endure,
  All weakness that impairs, all griefs that bow,
  Find their sole voice in that victorious brow.
MATTHEW ARNOLD

180

Since brass, nor stone, nor earth, nor boundless sea,
But sad mortality o'ersways their power,
How with this rage shall beauty hold a plea,
Whose action is no stronger than a flower?
O, how shall summer's honey breath hold out
Against the wreckful siege of battering days,
When rocks impregnable are not so stout,
Nor gates of steel so strong, but Time decays?
O fearful meditation! where, alack!
Shall Time's best jewel from Time's chest lie hid?
Or what strong hand can hold his swift foot back?
Or who his spoil of beauty can forbid?
  O, none, unless this miracle have might,
  That in black ink my love may still shine bright.
WILLIAM SHAKESPEARE

181 ## From *To the Memory of My Beloved, the Author, Mr. William Shakespeare*

Soul of the Age!
The applause, delight, the wonder of our stage!
My Shakespeare, rise. I will not lodge thee by
Chaucer or Spenser, or bid Beaumont lie

97   D

A little further to make thee a room;
  Thou art a monument without a tomb,
And art alive still while thy book doth live,
  And we have wits to read and praise to give. . . .
He was not of an age, but for all time! . . .
Yet must I not give Nature all; thy Art,
  My gentle Shakespeare, must enjoy a part.
For though the poet's matter Nature be,
  His art doth give the fashion. And that he
Who casts to write a living line must sweat,
  (Such as thine are) and strike the second heat
Upon the Muses' anvil; turn the same
  (And himself with it) that he thinks to frame;
Or for the laurel he may gain a scorn,
  For a good poet's made as well as born,
And such wert thou.

BEN JONSON

182   *Sappho to Anactoria*

Yea, thou shalt be forgotten like spilt wine,
Except these kisses of my lips on thine
Brand them with immortality; but me—
Men shall not see bright fire nor hear the sea,
Nor mix their hearts with music, nor behold
Cast forth of heaven with feet of awful gold
And plumeless wings that make the bright air blind,
Lightning, with thunder for a hound behind
Hunting through fields unfurrowed and unsown,
But in the light and laughter, in the moan
And music, and in grasp of lip and hand
And shudder of water that makes felt on land
The immeasurable tremor of all the sea,
Memories shall mix and metaphors of me. . . .
As a tear shed shalt thou be shed; but I—
Lo, earth may labour, men live long and die,
Years change and stars, and the high God devise
New things, and old things wane before his eyes
Who wields and wrecks them, being more strong than they—
But, having made me, me he shall not slay.

ALGERNON CHARLES SWINBURNE
(Anactoria)

When I have fears that I may cease to be
Before my pen has glean'd my teeming brain,
Before high-pilèd books, in charactery,
Hold like rich garners the full-ripen'd grain;
When I behold, upon the night's starr'd face,
Huge cloudy symbols of a high romance,
And feel that I may never live to trace
Their shadows, with the magic hand of chance;
And when I feel, fair creature of an hour,
That I shall never look upon thee more,
Never have relish in the faery power
Of unreflecting love;—then on the shore
  Of the wide world I stand alone, and think
  Till love and fame to nothingness do sink.

JOHN KEATS

184   *On the Death of Keats*

Peace, peace! he is not dead, he doth not sleep—
He hath awakened from the dream of life—
'Tis we who, lost in stormy visions, keep
With phantoms an unprofitable strife,
And in mad trance strike with our spirit's knife
Invulnerable nothings.—*We* decay
Like corpses in a charnel; fear and grief
Convulse us and consume us day by day,
And cold hopes swarm like worms within our living clay.

He has outsoared the shadow of our night;
Envy and calumny and hate and pain,
And that unrest which men miscall delight,
Can touch him not and torture not again;
From the contagion of the world's slow stain
He is secure, and now can never mourn
A heart grown cold, a head grown gray in vain;
Nor, when the spirit's self has ceased to burn,
With sparkless ashes load an unlamented urn. . . .

The One remains, the many change and pass;
Heaven's light forever shines, Earth's shadows fly;
Life, like a dome of many-coloured glass,
Stains the white radiance of Eternity,
Until Death tramples it to fragments.—Die,
If thou wouldst be with that which thou dost seek!
Follow where all is fled!—Rome's azure sky,
Flowers, ruins, statues, music, words are weak
The glory they transfuse with fitting truth to speak. . . .

The breath whose might I have invoked in song
Descends on me; my spirit's bark is driven,
Far from the shore, far from the trembling throng
Whose sails were never to the tempest given;
The massy earth and spherèd skies are riven!
I am borne darkly, fearfully, afar;
Whilst, burning through the inmost veil of Heaven,
The soul of Adonais, like a star,
Beacons from the abode where the Eternal are.

PERCY BYSSHE SHELLEY (*Adonais*)

185   From *Lycidas*

Alas! What boots it with incessant care
To tend the homely slighted shepherd's trade,
And strictly meditate the thankless Muse?
Were it not better done, as others use,
To sport with Amaryllis in the shade,
Or with the tangles of Neæra's hair?
Fame is the spur that the clear spirit doth raise
(That last infirmity of noble mind)
To scorn delights and live laborious days;
But the fair guerdon when we hope to find,
And think to burst out into sudden blaze,
Comes the blind Fury with th' abhorrèd shears,
And slits the thin spun life. 'But not the praise,'
Phoebus replied, and touched my trembling ears;
'Fame is no plant that grows on mortal soil,
Nor in the glistening foil

Set off to th' world, nor in broad rumour lies,
But lives and spreads aloft by those pure eyes,
And perfect witness of all-judging Jove;
As he pronounces lastly on each deed,
Of so much fame in Heav'n expect thy meed.' . . .

Weep no more, woeful shepherds, weep no more,
For Lycidas your sorrow, is not dead,
Sunk though he be beneath the watery floor.
So sinks the day-star in the ocean bed,
And yet anon repairs his drooping head,
And tricks his beams, and with new-spangled ore
Flames in the forehead of the morning sky:
So Lycidas sunk low, but mounted high,
Through the dear might of Him that walked the waves,
Where, other groves and other streams along,
With nectar pure his oozy locks he laves,
And hears the unexpressive nuptial song,
In the blest kingdoms meek of joy and love.
There entertain him all the saints above,
In solemn troops, and sweet societies
That sing, and singing in their glory move,
And wipe the tears for ever from his eyes.

JOHN MILTON

186   *The Future of English Poetry* (*1599*)

Or should we careless come behind the rest
    In power of words, that go before in worth,
    When as our accent's equal to the best,
    Is able greater wonders to bring forth:
    When all that ever hotter spirits expressed
    Comes bettered by the patience of the North?
And who in time knows whither we may vent
    The treasure of our tongue? To what strange shores
    This gain of our best glory shall be sent,
    T'enrich unknowing nations with our stores?
    What worlds in th' yet unformed Occident
    May come refined with th'accents that are ours?
Or who can tell for what great work in hand
    The greatness of our style is now ordained?

SAMUEL DANIEL (Musophilus)

187

If all the pens that ever poets held
Had fed the feeling of their masters' thoughts,
And every sweetness that inspir'd their hearts,
Their minds and muses on admirèd themes;
If all the heavenly quintessence they still
From their immortal flowers of poesy,
Wherein as in a mirror we perceive
The highest reaches of a human wit—
If these had made one poem's period,
And all combin'd in beauty's worthiness,
Yet should there hover in their restless heads
One thought, one grace, one wonder, at the least,
Which into words no virtue can digest.

CHRISTOPHER MARLOWE
(*Tamburlaine the Great*, First Part, V, 1)

188

Desiring this man's art, and that man's scope,
With what I most enjoy contented least.

WILLIAM SHAKESPEARE (*Sonnet* 29)

4

FANTASY AND SYMBOL

The opening passages are followed by songs, ballads and other poems which on the whole make use of northern, mediaeval or Christian folklore or legend, or of similar fantasies invented by the poets, rather than of Graeco-Roman mythology. But items 210–220 turn mainly on that mythology (which also serves the purposes of poets elsewhere in the anthology); and it continues to find a place at times in the succession (from 221 onwards) of earthly paradises and similar gardens or havens which poets have delighted to describe. The section ends with a more austere landscape, the symbolic 'red rock wilderness' of the poem written by Sidney Keyes in 1942 shortly before he was killed fighting in North Africa at the age of twenty:

> 'This is my calling, to seek the red rock desert
> And speak for all those who have lost the gardens,
> Forgotten the singing, yet dare not find the desert . . .'

---

189 From *Dream-Pedlary*

If there were dreams to sell,
  What would you buy?
Some cost a passing bell;
  Some a light sigh,
That shakes from Life's fresh crown
Only a rose-leaf down.
If there were dreams to sell,
Merry and sad to tell,
And the crier rang the bell,
  What would you buy?

THOMAS LOVELL BEDDOES

190

Lutes, laurels, seas of milk, and ships of amber.

THOMAS OTWAY (Venice Preserved, V, 1)

A sunny shaft did I behold,
  From sky to earth it slanted:
And poised therein a bird so bold—
  Sweet bird, thou wert enchanted!

He sank, he rose, he twinkled, he trolled
  Within that shaft of sunny mist;
His eyes of fire, his beak of gold,
  All else of amethyst!

And thus he sang: 'Adieu! adieu!
Love's dreams prove seldom true.
The blossoms, they make no delay:
The sparkling dew-drops will not stay.
  Sweet month of May,
   We must away;
   Far, far away!
    To-day! to-day!'
SAMUEL TAYLOR COLERIDGE *(Zapolya)*

192

And airy tongues that syllable men's names
On sands and shores and desert wildernesses.
JOHN MILTON *(Comus)*

193

    He ne'er is crowned
With immortality, who fears to follow
Where airy voices lead.
JOHN KEATS *(Endymion*, II)

194   From *Thomas the Rhymer*

True Thomas lay on Huntlie bank;
  A ferlie he spied wi' his e'e;
And there he saw a lady bright
  Come riding down by Eildon Tree.

Her skirt was o' the grass-green silk,
  Her mantle o' the velvet fine;
At ilka tett o' her horse's mane
  Hung fifty siller bells and nine.

True Thomas he pull'd off his cap,
  And louted low down on his knee:
'Hail to thee, Mary, Queen of Heaven!
  For thy peer on earth I never did see.'

'O no, O no, Thomas,' she said,
  'That name does not belang to me;
I'm but the Queen o' fair Elfland,
  That am hither come to visit thee. . . .

'O see ye not yon narrow road,
  So thick beset wi' thorns and briars?
That is the Path of Righteousness,
  Though after it but few inquires.

'And see ye not yon braid, braid road,
  That lies across the lily leven?
That is the Path of Wickedness,
  Though some call it the Road to Heaven.

'And see ye not yon bonny road
  That winds about the fernie brae?
That is the Road to fair Elfland,
  Where thou and I this night maun gae.'

ANONYMOUS

195   *The Outskirts*

The night was cloyed with flowers
In the darkness deep and sweet,
When, at the window of the World,
I heard the dancing feet;
And viol and tambour
Made musical the air,
While yet a voice within me cried,
        Beware!

My eyes upon the glow were set
From out that thorny grot:
I hungered for the lips and eyes
And hearts remembering not;
And still the thrill and thud beat on
With sorcery in the air;
And, luring, leaping, called to me,
      Beware!

O all you hapless souls, like birds
Within night's branching may,
Hearken the words of him who speaks,
And fly from hence—away.
These dancers with their wiles and gauds,
That music on the air—
'Tis the swart Fowler with his nets
To play you false, though fair;
Hearken—an outcast I—I cry,
      Beware!

WALTER DE LA MARE

196   *La Belle Dame sans Merci*

O what can ail thee, knight-at-arms,
  Alone and palely loitering?
The sedge has withered from the lake,
  And no birds sing.

O what can ail thee, knight-at-arms,
  So haggard and so woe-begone?
The squirrel's granary is full,
  And the harvest's done.

I see a lily on thy brow
  With anguish moist and fever dew,
And on thy cheeks a fading rose
  Fast withereth too.

I met a lady in the meads,
  Full beautiful—a faery's child;
Her hair was long, her foot was light,
  And her eyes were wild.

I made a garland for her head,
  And bracelets too, and fragrant zone;
She look'd at me as she did love,
  And made sweet moan.

I set her on my pacing steed,
  And nothing else saw all day long,
For sidelong would she bend, and sing
  A faery's song.

She found me roots of relish sweet,
  And honey wild, and manna dew,
And sure in language strange she said,
  'I love thee true!'

She took me to her elfin grot,
  And there she wept and sighed full sore,
And there I shut her wild, wild eyes
  With kisses four.

And there she lullèd me asleep,
  And there I dream'd—ah, woe betide!
The latest dream I ever dream'd
  On the cold hill's side.

I saw pale kings and princes too,
  Pale warriors, death-pale were they all;
They cried—'La Belle Dame sans Merci
  Hath thee in thrall!'

I saw their starved lips in the gloam,
  With horrid warning gapèd wide,
And I awoke and found me here,
  On the cold hill's side.

And this is why I sojourn here,
  Alone and palely loitering,
Though the sedge is wither'd from the lake,
  And no birds sing.

JOHN KEATS

But oh! that deep romantic chasm which slanted
Down the green hill athwart a cedarn cover!
A savage place! as holy and enchanted
As e'er beneath a waning moon was haunted
By woman wailing for her demon-lover!

SAMUEL TAYLOR COLERIDGE (*Kubla Khan*)

198   ## Janet Wins Her Lover Back from
Fairyland

Janet has kilted her green kirtle
    A little abune the knee;
And she has snooded her yellow hair
    A little abune her bree,
And she is on to Miles Cross
    As fast as she can hie.

About the dead hour o' the night
    She heard the bridles ring;
And Janet was as glad at that
    As any earthly thing.

And first gaed by the black, black steed,
    And syne gaed by the brown;
But fast she gript the milk-white steed
    And pu'd the rider down.

She's pu'd him frae the milk-white steed,
    An loot the bridle fa',
And up there rase an eldritch cry,
    'True Tam Lin he's awa'!'

They shaped him in her arms twa
    An aske but and a snake;
But aye she grips and hau'ds him fast
    To be her warldis make.

They shaped him in her arms twa
　　But and a deer sae wild;
But aye she grips and hau'ds him fast,
　　The father o' her child.

They shaped him in her arms twa
　　A hot iron at the fire;
But aye she grips and hau'ds him fast
　　To be her heart's desire.

They shaped him in her arms at last
　　A mother-naked man;
She cast her mantle over him,
　　And sae her love she wan. . . .

Out then spak' the Queen o' Fairies,
　　And an angry woman was she,
'She's ta'en awa' the bonniest knight
　　In a' my companie!'

ANONYMOUS　(Tam Lin)

199　*Amor Mundi*

'Oh where are you going with your love-locks flowing,
　　On the west wind blowing along this valley track?'
'The downhill path is easy, come with me an it please ye,
　　We shall escape the uphill by never turning back.'

.　　　.　　　.　　　.

'Oh what is that in heaven where grey cloud-flakes are seven'
　　Where blackest clouds hang riven just at the rainy skirt?,
'Oh that's a meteor sent us, a message dumb, portentous,
　　An undeciphered solemn signal of help or hurt.'

'Oh what is that glides quickly where velvet flowers grow
　　thickly,
　　Their scent comes rich and sickly?' 'A scaled and hooded
　　worm.'
'Oh what's that in the hollow, so pale I quake to follow?'
　　'Oh that's a thin dead body which waits the eternal term.'

'Turn again, O my sweetest,—turn again, false and fleetest:
 This beaten way thou beatest, I fear, is hell's own track.'
'Nay, too steep for hill mounting; nay, too late for cost
    counting:
 This downhill path is easy, but there's no turning back.'

CHRISTINA GEORGINA ROSSETTI

200

'O where are you going?' said reader to rider,
'That valley is fatal when furnaces burn,
Yonder's the midden whose odours will madden,
That gap is the grave where the tall return.'

'O do you imagine,' said fearer to farer,
'That dusk will delay on your path to the pass,
Your diligent looking discover the lacking
Your footsteps feel from granite to grass?'

'O what was that bird?' said horror to hearer,
'Did you see that shape in the twisted trees?
Behind you swiftly the figure comes softly,
The spot on your skin is a shocking disease.'

'Out of this house'—said rider to reader
'Yours never will'—said farer to fearer
'They're looking for you'—said hearer to horror
As he left them there, as he left them there.

WYSTAN HUGH AUDEN
(Epilogue from The Orators)

201   The End of a Murderer

(The priest, Caponsacchi, on Count Guido)

So I lose Guido in the loneliness,
Silence and dusk, till at the doleful end,
At the horizontal line, creation's verge,
From what just is to absolute nothingness—

Whom is it, straining onward still, he meets?
What other man deep further in the fate,
Who, turning at the prize of a footfall
To flatter him and promise fellowship,
Discovers in the act a frightful face—
Judas, made monstrous by much solitude!
The two are at one now! Let them love their love
That bites and claws like hate, or hate their hate
That mops and mows and makes as it were love!
There, let them tear each other in devil's-fun,
Or fondle this the other while malice aches—
Both teach, both learn detestability!
Kiss him the kiss, Iscariot! . . .
There let them grapple, denizens o' the dark,
Foes or friends, but indissolubly bound,
In their one spot out of the ken of God
Or care of man, for ever and ever more!

ROBERT BROWNING

(*The Ring and the Book*, VI)

202   *After the French Revolution*

Saint Peter sat by the celestial gate:
   His keys were rusty, and the lock was dull,
So little trouble had been given of late;
   Not that the place by any means was full,
But since the Gallic era 'eighty-eight'
   The devils had ta'en a longer, stronger pull,
And 'a pull altogether,' as they say
At sea—which drew most souls another way.

The angels all were singing out of tune,
   And hoarse with having little else to do,
Excepting to wind up the sun and moon
   Or curb a runaway young star or two,
Or wild colt of a comet, which too soon
   Broke out of bounds o'er the ethereal blue,
Splitting some planet with its playful tail,
As boats are sometimes by a wanton whale.

The guardian seraphs had retired on high,
    Finding their charges past all care below;
Terrestrial business fill'd nought in the sky
    Save the recording angel's black bureau;
Who found, indeed, the facts to multiply
    With such rapidity of vice and woe,
That he had stripp'd off both his wings in quills,
And yet was in arrear of human ills.

LORD BYRON (*The Vision of Judgement*)

203

I long to talk with some old lover's ghost
    Who died before the god of love was born.
JOHN DONNE (*Love's Deity*)

204   *Keith of Ravelston*

The murmur of the mourning ghost
    That keeps the shadowy kine,
'O Keith of Ravelston,
    The sorrows of thy line!'

Ravelston, Ravelston,
    The merry path that leads
Down the golden morning hill,
    And thro' the silver meads;

Ravelston, Ravelston,
    The stile beneath the tree,
The maid that kept her mother's kine,
    The song that sang she!

She sang her song, she kept her kine,
    She sat beneath the thorn,
When Andrew Keith of Ravelston
    Rode thro' the Monday morn.

His henchmen sing, his hawk-bells ring,
    His belted jewels shine;
O Keith of Ravelston,
    The sorrows of thy line!

Year after year, where Andrew came,
  Comes evening down the glade,
And still there sits a moonshine ghost
  Where sat the sunshine maid.

Her misty hair is faint and fair,
  She keeps the shadowy kine;
O Keith of Ravelston,
  The sorrows of thy line!

I lay my hand upon the stile,
  The stile is lone and cold,
The burnie that goes babbling by
  Says naught that can be told.

Yet, stranger! here, from year to year,
  She keeps her shadowy kine;
O Keith of Ravelston,
  The sorrows of thy line!

Step out three steps where Andrew stood—
  Why blanch thy cheeks for fear?
The ancient stile is not alone,
  'Tis not the burn I hear!

She makes her immemorial moan,
  She keeps her shadowy kine;
O Keith of Ravelston,
  The sorrows of thy line!

SYDNEY DOBELL

205   *In the Hebrides*

Unbounded is thy range; with varied style
  Thy Muse may, like those feath'ry tribes which spring
From their rude rocks, extend her skirting wing
  Round the moist marge of each cold Hebrid isle,
To that hoar pile which still its ruins shows:
  In whose small vaults a pigmy-folk is found,
Whose bones the delver with his spade upthrows,
  And culls them, wond'ring, from the hallow'd ground!

Or thither where beneath the show'ry west
   The mighty kings of three fair realms are laid;
Once foes, perhaps, together now they rest.
   No slaves revere them, and no wars invade:
Yet frequent now, at midnight's solemn hour,
   The rifted mounds their yawning cells unfold,
And forth the monarchs stalk with sov'reign pow'r
   In pageant robes, and wreath'd with sheeny gold,
And on their twilight tombs aërial council hold.

WILLIAM COLLINS (*Ode on the Popular Super-*
stitions of the Highlands of Scotland)

206

Ere Babylon was dust,
The Magus Zoroaster, my dear child,
Met his own image walking in the garden.
That apparition, sole of men, he saw.
For know, there are two worlds of life and death:
One that which thou beholdest; but the other
Is underneath the grave, where do inhabit
The shadows of all forms that think and live
Till death unite them and they part no more;
Dreams and the light imaginings of men,
And all that faith creates or love desires,
Terrible, strange, sublime and beauteous shapes.

PERCY BYSSHE SHELLEY
(*Prometheus Unbound*, I)

207   From *Love's Nocturn*

Vaporous, unaccountable,
   Dreamland lies forlorn of light,
Hollow like a breathing shell . . .

Poet's fancies all are there:
   There the elf-girls flood with wings
Valleys full of plaintive air;

There breathe perfumes; there in rings
Whirl the foam-bewildered springs;
    Siren there
Winds her dizzy hair and sings . . .

Reft of her, my dreams are all
    Clammy trance that fears the sky:
Changing footpaths shift and fall;
    From polluted coverts nigh
    Miserable phantoms sigh;
        Quakes the pall
And the funeral goes by . . .

Darkness and the breath of space
    Like loud waters everywhere. . . .

DANTE GABRIEL ROSSETTI

208   From *Tom o' Bedlam's Song*

The moon's my constant mistress
And the lowly owl my morrow;
    The flaming drake
    And the night-crow make
Me music to my sorrow . . .

I know more than Apollo,
For oft, when he lies sleeping,
    I see the stars
    At bloody wars
In the wounded welkin weeping,
The moon embrace her shepherd
And the queen of love her warrior,
    While the first doth horn
    The star of the morn
And the next the heavenly farrier. . . .

With a heart of furious fancies
Whereof I am commander,
    With a burning spear
    And a horse of air

To the wilderness I wander;
By a knight of ghosts and shadows
I summoned am to tourney
   Ten leagues beyond
   The wide world's end
—Methinks it is no journey.

ANONYMOUS

209

How crude and sore
The journey homeward to habitual self.

JOHN KEATS (Endymion, II)

210

The world is too much with us; late and soon,
   Getting and spending, we lay waste our powers:
   Little we see in Nature that is ours;
We have given our hearts away, a sordid boon!
This sea that bares her bosom to the moon;
   The winds that will be howling at all hours,
   And are up-gather'd now like sleeping flowers;
For this, for everything, we are out of tune;
It moves us not.—Great God! I'd rather be
   A Pagan suckled in a creed outworn;
So might I, standing on this pleasant lea,
   Have glimpses that would make me less forlorn;
Have sight of Proteus rising from the sea;
   Or hear old Triton blow his wreathèd horn.

WILLIAM WORDSWORTH

211   *In a Monastery of the Carthusians*

Not as their friend or child I speak!
But as on some far northern strand,
Thinking of his own Gods, a Greek
In pity and mournful awe might stand
Before some fallen Runic stone—
For both were faiths, and both are gone.

Wandering between two worlds, one dead,
The other powerless to be born,
With nowhere yet to rest my head,
Like these, on earth I wait forlorn.
Their faith, my tears, the world deride;
I come to shed them at their side.

MATTHEW ARNOLD
(*Stanzas from the Grande Chartreuse*)

212   ## To the Muses

Whether on Ida's shady brow,
Or in the chambers of the East,
The chambers of the sun, that now
From ancient melody have ceas'd;

Whether in Heaven ye wander fair,
Or the green corners of the earth,
Or the blue regions of the air
Where the melodious winds have birth;

Whether on crystal rocks ye rove,
Beneath the bosom of the sea
Wand'ring in many a coral grove,
Fair Nine, forsaking Poetry!

How have you left the ancient love
That bards of old enjoy'd in you!
The languid strings do scarcely move!
The sound is forced, the notes are few!

WILLIAM BLAKE

213

Shake off your heavy trance!
    And leap into a dance
Such as no mortals use to tread:
    Fit only for Apollo
To play to, for the moon to lead,
    And all the stars to follow!

FRANCIS BEAUMONT
(*The Masque of the Inner Temple*)

From the forests and highlands
    We come, we come;
From the river-girt islands,
    Where loud waves are dumb,
Listening to my sweet pipings.
      The wind in the reeds and the rushes,
        The bees on the bells of thyme,
      The birds on the myrtle bushes,
        The cicale above in the lime,
And the lizards below in the grass,
Were as silent as ever old Tmolus was,
    Listening to my sweet pipings.

Liquid Peneus was flowing,
    And all dark Tempe lay
In Pelion's shadow, outgrowing
    The light of the dying day,
Speeded by my sweet pipings.
      The Sileni and Sylvans and Fauns,
        And the Nymphs of the woods and waves,
      To the edge of the moist river-lawns,
        And the brink of the dewy caves,
And all that did then attend and follow,
Were silent with love, as you now, Apollo,
    With envy of my sweet pipings.

I sang of the dancing stars,
    I sang of the dædal earth,
And of heaven, and the giant wars,
    And love, and death, and birth.
And then I changed my pipings—
      Singing how down the vale of Mænalus
        I pursued a maiden, and clasp'd a reed:
      Gods and men, we are all deluded thus;
        It breaks in our bosom, and then we bleed.
All wept—as I think both ye now would,
If envy or age had not frozen your blood—
    At the sorrow of my sweet pipings.

PERCY BYSSHE SHELLEY

Whispering I knew not what of wild and sweet,
Like that strange song I heard Apollo sing,
While Ilion like a mist rose into towers.

ALFRED, LORD TENNYSON (*Tithonus*)

216

Fairest of fair, O lady mine, Venus . . .
Thou gladder of the mount of Citheron.

GEOFFREY CHAUCER (*The Knight's Tale*)

217   *The God of the North Wind Seizes*
Oreithyia

With a leap of his limbs as a lion's, a cry from his lips as
    of thunder,
  In a storm of amorous godhead filled with fire,
From the height of the heaven that was rent with the roar
    of his coming in sunder,
  Sprang the strong God on the spoil of his desire.
  And the pines of the hills were as green reeds shattered,
  And their branches as buds of the soft spring scattered,
  And the west wind and east, and the sound of the south,
  Fell dumb at the blast of the north wind's mouth,
    At the cry of his coming out of heaven.
  And the wild beasts quailed in the rifts and hollows
  Where hound nor clarion of huntsman follows,
  And the depths of the sea were aghast, and whitened,
  And the crowns of their waves were as flame that
    lightened,
    And the heart of the floods thereof was riven.
But she knew not him coming for terror, she felt not her
    wrong that he wrought her,
  When her locks as leaves were shed before his breath,
And she heard not for terror his prayer, though the cry
    was a God's that besought her,
  Blown from lips that strew the world-wide seas with death.

For the heart was molten within her to hear,
And her knees beneath her were loosened for fear,
And her blood fast bound as a frost-bound water,
And the soft new bloom of the green earth's daughter
   Wind-wasted as blossom of a tree;
As the wild God rapt her from earth's breast lifted,
On the strength of the stream of his dark breath drifted,
From the bosom of earth as a bride from the mother,
With storm for bridesman and wreck for brother
   As a cloud that he sheds upon the sea.

     ALGERNON CHARLES SWINBURNE *(Erechtheus)*

218

But ah! in vain my restless feet
Traced every silent shady seat
   Which knew their forms of old:
Nor Naiad, by her fountain laid,
Nor Wood-nymph, tripping through her glade,
   Did now their rites unfold;

Whether to nurse some infant oak
They turn the slowly tinkling brook,
   And catch the pearly showers;
Or brush the mildew from the woods,
Or paint with noontide beams the birds,
   Or breathe on opening flowers.

      MARK AKENSIDE
     (To the Honourable Charles Townsend)

219 From *Ode on the Morning of Christ's Nativity*

The oracles are dumb,
No voice or hideous hum
   Runs through the archèd roof in words deceiving.
Apollo from his shrine
Can no more divine,
   With hollow shriek the steep of Delphos leaving.
No nightly trance, or breathèd spell,
Inspires the pale-ey'd priest from the prophetic cell.

The lonely mountains o'er,
And the resounding shore,
   A voice of weeping heard, and loud lament;
From haunted spring and dale,
Edg'd with poplar pale,
   The parting Genius is with sighing sent;
With flower-inwoven tresses torn
The Nymphs in twilight shade of tangled thickets mourn.

JOHN MILTON

220

The intelligible forms of ancient poets,
The fair humanities of old religion,
The power, the beauty and the majesty
That had their haunts in dale or piny mountain
Or forest, by slow stream or pebbly spring
Or chasms and watery depths; all these have vanished,
They live no longer in the faith of reason:
But still the heart doth need a language, still
Doth the old instinct bring back the old names.

SAMUEL TAYLOR COLERIDGE, after SCHILLER
(*Piccolomini*, II, 4)

221   From *The Earthly Paradise*

Dreamer of dreams, born out of my due time,
Why should I strive to set the crooked straight? . . .
Who strive to build a shadowy isle of bliss
Midmost the beating of the steely sea.

WILLIAM MORRIS

222   *Inscription Over a Gate*

Through me men go into that blissful place
Of hertë's heal and deadly woundës' cure;
Through me men go unto the well of Grace,
There green and lusty May shall ever endure.
This is the way to all good aventure.

GEOFFREY CHAUCER
(*The Parliament of Fowls*)

121

There is continual spring, and harvest there
Continual, both meeting at one time:
For both the boughs do laughing blossoms bear,
And with fresh colours deck the wanton prime,
And eke at once the heavy trees they climb,
Which seem to labour under their fruit's load:
The whiles the joyous birds make their pastime
Amongst the shady leaves, their sweet abode,
And their true loves without suspicion tell abroad.

Right in the middest of that Paradise,
There stood a stately Mount, on whose round top
A gloomy grove of myrtle trees did rise,
Whose shady boughs sharp steel did never lop,
Nor wicked beasts their tender buds did crop,
But like a garland compassèd the height,
And from their fruitful sides sweet gum did drop,
That all the ground with precious dew bedight,
Threw forth most dainty odours, and most sweet delight. . . .

There wont fair Venus often to enjoy
Her dear Adonis joyous company.
         . . . In secret he does lie
Lappèd in flowers and precious spicery.

         EDMUND SPENSER   (*The Faery Queen*, VII, 6)

224

Be not afeard; the isle is full of noises,
Sounds, and sweet airs, that give delight and hurt not.
Sometimes a thousand twangling instruments
Will hum about mine ears; and sometimes voices
That, if I then had waked after long sleep,
Will make me sleep again; and then, in dreaming,
The clouds, methought, would open and shew riches
Ready to drop upon me: that when I waked,
I cried to dream again.

         WILLIAM SHAKESPEARE
            (*The Tempest*, III, 2)

The Garden of Eden

Adam and Eve in Paradise

Groves whose rich trees wept odorous gums and balm,
Others whose fruit, burnished with golden rind,
Hung amiable—Hesperian fables true,
If true, here only—and of delicious taste.
Betwixt them lawns, or level downs, and flocks
Grazing the tender herb, were interposed,
Or palmy hillock, or the flowery lap
Of some irriguous valley spread her store,
Flowers of all hue, and without thorn the rose.
Another side, umbrageous grots and caves
Of cool recess, o'er which the mantling vine
Lays forth her purple grape, and gently creeps
Luxuriant; meanwhile murmuring waters fall
Down the slope hills, dispersed, or in a lake,
That to the fringèd bank with myrtle crowned
Her crystal mirror holds, unite their streams.
The birds their choir apply; airs, vernal airs,
Breathing the smell of field and grove, attune
The trembling leaves, while universal Pan,
Knit with the Graces and the Hours in dance,
Led on th' eternal spring. Not that fair field
Of Enna, where Proserpin gathering flowers,
Herself a fairer flower, by gloomy Dis
Was gathered—which cost Ceres all that pain
To seek her through the world—nor that sweet grove
Of Daphne by Orontes, and th' inspired
Castalian spring might with this Paradise
Of Eden strive.

Paradise Lost

In either hand the hastening Angel caught
Our ling'ring parents, and to the eastern gate
Led them direct, and down the cliff as fast
To the subjected plain; then disappeared.
They looking back, all the eastern side beheld
Of Paradise, so late their happy seat,
Waved over by that flaming brand, the gate
With dreadful faces thronged and fiery arms.

Some natural tears they dropped, but wiped them soon;
The world was all before them, where to choose
Their place of rest, and Providence their guide.
They, hand in hand, with wandering steps and slow,
Through Eden took their solitary way.

Eden After the Deluge

Then shall this mount
Of paradise by might of waves be moved
Out of his place, pushed by the hornèd flood,
With all his verdure spoiled, and trees adrift
Down the great river to the opening gulf,
And there take root, an island salt and bare,
The haunt of seals, and orcs, and sea-mews' clang.

JOHN MILTON
(*Paradise Lost*, IV, XII, XI)

226   From *The Castle of Indolence*

And there a season atween June and May,
Half prankt with spring, with summer half imbrowned,
A listless climate made, where, sooth to say,
No living wight could work, ne carèd even for play.

Was nought around but images of rest:
Sleep-soothing groves, and quiet lawns between;
And flowery beds that slumbrous influence kest,
From poppies breathed; and beds of pleasant green,
Where never yet was creeping creature seen.
Meantime unnumbered glittering streamlets played,
And hurlèd everywhere their waters sheen;
That, as they bickered through the sunny glade,
Though restless still themselves, a lulling murmur made. . . .

A pleasing land of drowsyhead it was:
Of dreams that wave before the half-shut eye,
And of gay castles in the clouds that pass,
For ever flushing round a summer sky:
There eke the soft delights, that witchingly

Instil a wanton sweetness through the breast,
And the calm pleasures always hovered nigh;
But whate'er smacked of noyance, or unrest,
Was far far off expelled from this delicious nest.

JAMES THOMSON

227 *Song*

Christ keep the Hollow Land
    All the summer-tide;
Still we cannot understand
    Where the waters glide;

Only dimly seeing them
    Coldly slipping through
Many green-lipped cavern mouths
    Where the hills are blue.

WILLIAM MORRIS

228 *Heaven-Haven*

A Nun Takes the Veil

I have desired to go
    Where springs not fail,
To fields where flies no sharp and sided hail
    And a few lilies blow.

And I have asked to be
    Where no storms come,
Where the green swell is in the havens dumb,
    And out of the swing of the sea.

GERARD MANLEY HOPKINS

229 *Arabia*

Far are the shades of Arabia,
    Where the Princes ride at noon,
'Mid the verdurous vales and thickets,
    Under the ghost of the moon;

And so dark is that vaulted purple,
    Flowers in the forest rise
And toss into blossom 'gainst the phantom stars
    Pale in the noonday skies.

Sweet is the music of Arabia
    In my heart, when out of dreams
I still in the thin clear mirk of dawn
    Descry her gliding streams;
Hear her strange lutes on the green banks
    Ring loud with the grief and delight
Of the dim-silked, dark-haired Musicians
    In the brooding silence of night.

They haunt me—her lutes and her forests;
    No beauty on earth I see
But shadowed with that dream recalls
    Her loveliness to me:
Still eyes look coldly upon me,
    Cold voices whisper and say—
'He is crazed with the spell of far Arabia,
    They have stolen his wits away.'

              WALTER DE LA MARE

230   *The Phœnix*

O blest unfabled Incense Tree,
That burns in glorious Araby,
With red scent chalicing the air,
Till earth-life grow Elysian there!

Half buried to her flaming breast
In this bright tree, she makes her nest,
Hundred-sunned Phoenix! when she must
Crumble at length to hoary dust!

Her gorgeous death-bed! her rich pyre
Burnt up with aromatic fire!
Her urn, sight high from spoiler men!
Her birthplace when self-born again!

The mountainless green wilds among,
Here ends she her unechoing song!
With amber tears and odorous sighs
Mourned by the desert where she dies!

Laid like the young fawn mossily
In sun-green vales of Araby,
I woke hard by the Phoenix tree
That with shadeless boughs flamed over me,
And upward called by a dumb cry
With moonbroad orbs of wonder, I
Beheld the immortal Bird on high
Glassing the great sun in her eye . . .
Slowly to crimson embers turn
The beauties of the brightsome one.
O'er the broad nest her silver wings
Shook down their wasteful glitterings;
Her brinded neck high-arched in air
Like a small rainbow faded there;
But brighter glowed her plumy crown
Mouldering to golden ashes down; . . .
The while with shrill triumphant tone
Sounding aloud, aloft, alone,
Ceaseless her joyful deathwail she
Sang to departing Araby!

GEORGE DARLEY (*Nepenthe*)

231   From *The Wilderness*

The red rock wilderness
Shall be my dwelling-place.

Where the wind saws at the bluffs
And the pebble falls like thunder
I shall watch the clawed sun
Tear the rocks asunder.

The seven-branched cactus
Will never sweat wine:
My own bleeding feet
Shall furnish the sign.

The rock says 'Endure.'
The wind says 'Pursue.'
The sun says 'I will suck your bones
And afterwards bury you.'

. . . .

I am content to face the destroying sun.
There shall be no more journeys, nor the anguish
Of meeting and parting, after the last great parting
From the images of dancing and the gardens
Where the brown bird chokes in its song:
Until that last great meeting among mountains
Where the metal bird sings madly.from the fire.

. . . .

In this hard garden where the earth's ribs
Lie bare from her first agony, I seek
The home of the gold bird, the predatory Phoenix.
O louder than the tongue of any river
Call the red flames among the shapes of rock:
And this is my calling. . . .
                    Though my love must sit
Alone with her candle in a darkened room
Listening to music that is not present or
Turning a flower in her childish hands
And though we were a thousand miles apart . . .
This is my calling, to seek the red rock desert
And speak for all those who have lost the gardens,
Forgotten the singing, yet dare not find the desert—
To sing the song that rises from the fire.

. . . .

There is no parting
From friends, but only from the ways of friendship;
Nor from our lovers, though the forms of love
Change often as the landscape of this journey
To the dark valley where the gold bird burns.
I say, Love is a wilderness and these bones
Proclaim no failure, but the death of youth.

We say, You must be ready for the desert
Even among the orchards starred with blossom,
Even in spring, or at the waking moment
When the man turns to the woman, and both are afraid.
All who would save their life must find the desert—
The lover, the poet, the girl who dreams of Christ,
And the swift runner, crowned with another laurel:
They all must face the sun, the red rock desert,
And see the burning of the metal bird.
Until you have crossed the desert and faced that fire
Love is an evil, a shaking of the hand,
A sick pain draining courage from the heart.

SIDNEY KEYES

5

MAN AND NATURE

The earth in the cosmic environment is revealed by the night-sky with the heavenly bodies, including, in A. E. Housman's phrase, 'that patroness of poets, the moon.' With uneasiness or triumph, man has tried to understand what he has seen outside the earth and on the earth (244–250). Apart from the adventures at sea described in *Action*, he has considered with varying feelings the sea, her inhabitants, and her borders. From item 260 onwards, the poetry relates to earth's zones of arctic or northern wastes and high mountain ranges, or to climates of heat, drought, or rain, together with the creatures which live in or visit such parts of the world. Thereafter (280–302) we see the trees and flowers, and trace the progress of the seasons, in temperate and cultivated regions like the British Isles. The section closes with general poems on man and nature, or on the future of his planet.

---

232   *At a Lunar Eclipse*

Thy shadow, Earth, from Pole to Central Sea,
Now steals along upon the Moon's meek shine
In even monochrome and curving line
Of imperturbable serenity.

How shall I link such sun-cast symmetry
With the torn troubled form I know as thine,
That profile, placid as a brow divine,
With continents of moil and misery?

And can immense Mortality but throw
So small a shade, and Heaven's high human scheme
Be hemmed within the coasts yon arc implies?

Is such a stellar gauge of earthly show,
Nation at war with nation, brains that teem,
Heroes, and women fairer than the skies?

THOMAS HARDY

Mysterious Night! when our first parent knew
Thee from report divine, and heard thy name,
Did he not tremble for this lovely frame,
This glorious canopy of light and blue?
Yet 'neath a curtain of translucent dew,
Bathed in the rays of the great setting flame,
Hesperus with the host of heaven came,
And lo! creation widened in man's view.
Who could have thought such darkness lay concealed
Within thy beams, O Sun! or who could find,
Whilst flow'r and leaf and insect stood revealed,
That to such countless orbs thou mad'st us blind?
  Why do we then shun Death with anxious strife?
  If Light can thus deceive, wherefore not Life?

JOSEPH BLANCO WHITE

234   *The Moon Rises Over Eden*

         Now glowed the firmament
With living sapphires: Hesperus that led
The starry host, rode brightest, till the moon,
Rising in clouded majesty, at length
Apparent queen unveiled her peerless light,
And o'er the dark her silver mantle threw.

JOHN MILTON (*Paradise Lost*, IV)

235   *To the Moon*

  Art thou pale for weariness
Of climbing heaven and gazing on the earth,
Wandering companionless
Among the stars that have a different birth,—
And ever changing, like a joyless eye
That finds no object worth its constancy?

PERCY BYSSHE SHELLEY

With how sad steps, O Moon, thou climb'st the skies!
How silently, and with how wan a face!
What! may it be that even in heavenly place
That busy archer his sharp arrows tries?
Sure, if that long-with-love-acquainted eyes
Can judge of love, thou feel'st a lover's case:
I read it in thy looks; thy languished grace
To me, that feel the like, thy state descries.
Then, even of fellowship, O Moon, tell me,
Is constant love deemed there but want of wit?
Are beauties there as proud as here they be?
Do they above love to be loved, and yet
Those lovers scorn whom that love doth possess?
Do they call virtue there—ungratefulness?

SIR PHILIP SIDNEY

A comet glittered in the air of late,
And kept some weeks the frightened kingdom waking.
Long hair it had, like you; a shining aspect;
Its beauty smiled, at the same time it frightened;
And every horror in it had a grace.

JOHN CROWNE (*The Ambitious Statesman*, III)

238   From *November*

Look out upon the real world, where the moon,
Half-way 'twixt root and crown of these high trees,
Turns the dead midnight into dreamy noon. . . .
Is it not fair, and of most wondrous worth?

Yea, I have looked, and seen November there:
The changeless seal of change it seemed to be,
Fair death of things that, living once, were fair;
Bright sign of loneliness too great for me,
Strange image of the dread eternity,
In whose void patience how can these have part,
These outstretched feverish hands, this restless heart?

WILLIAM MORRIS (*The Earthly Paradise*)

Look how the floor of heaven
Is thick inlaid with patines of bright gold;
There's not the smallest orb which thou behold'st
But in his motion like an angel sings,
Still quiring to the young-eyed cherubims.

WILLIAM SHAKESPEARE

(*The Merchant of Venice*, V, 1)

240

Silent, silent Night,
Quench the holy light
Of thy torches bright.

WILLIAM BLAKE (*Silent, silent Night*)

241

Hark! hark! the lark at heaven's gate sings,
    And Phoebus 'gins arise,
His steeds to water at those springs
    On chaliced flowers that lies;
And winking Mary-buds begin
    To ope their golden eyes:
With everything that pretty is,
    My lady sweet, arise!
        Arise, arise!

WILLIAM SHAKESPEARE

(*Cymbeline*, II, 3)

242

The busy larkë, messager of day,
Saluëth in her song the morrow gray,
And fiery Phoebus riseth up so bright
That all the orient laugheth of the light.

GEOFFREY CHAUCER (*The Knight's Tale*)

See, the dapple grey coursers of the morn
Beat up the light with their bright silver hooves
And chase it through the sky.

JOHN MARSTON (*Antonio and Mellida*, I, 1)

244

New philosophy calls all in doubt;
The element of fire is quite put out:
The sun is lost, and the earth, and no man's wit
Can well direct him where to look for it.
And freely men confess that this world's spent,
When in the planets, and the firmament,
They seek so many new; they see that this
Is crumbled out again to his atomies.
'Tis all in pieces, all coherence gone,
All just supply, and all relation.

JOHN DONNE
(*An Anatomy of the World: The First Anniversary*)

245

Nature, that fram'd us of four elements
Warring within our breasts for regiment,
Doth teach us all to have aspiring minds;
Our souls, whose faculties can comprehend
The wondrous architecture of the world,
And measure every wandering planet's course,
Still climbing after knowledge infinite,
And always moving as the restless spheres,
Will us to wear ourselves and never rest,
Until we reach the ripest fruit of all. . . .

CHRISTOPHER MARLOWE
(*Tamburlaine the Great*, First Part, II, 7)

Through seas of knowledge, we our course advance,
Discov'ring still new worlds of ignorance.

SIR JOHN DENHAM
(*The Progress of Learning*)

247   *A Statue of Newton at Cambridge*

Newton, with his prism and silent face,
The marble index of a mind for ever
Voyaging through strange seas of Thought, alone.

WILLIAM WORDSWORTH (*The Prelude*, III)

248   *Epitaph for Newton*

Nature and Nature's laws lay hid in night:
God said, *Let Newton be!* and all was light.

ALEXANDER POPE

249

There rolls the deep where grew the tree.
   O earth, what changes hast thou seen!
   There, where the long street roars, hath been
The stillness of the central sea.

The hills are shadows, and they flow
   From form to form, and nothing stands;
   They melt like mist, the solid lands,
Like clouds they shape themselves and go.

ALFRED, LORD TENNYSON
(*In Memoriam*, cxxiii)

250

The centre-fire heaves underneath the earth,
And the earth changes like a human face;
The molten ore bursts up among the rocks,
Winds into the stone's heart, outbranches bright

In hidden mines, spots barren river-beds,
Crumbles into fine sand where sunbeams bask—
God joys therein. The wroth sea's waves are edged
With foam, white as the bitten lip of hate,
When, in the solitary waste, strange groups
Of young volcanoes come up, cyclops-like,
Staring together with their eyes on flame.

ROBERT BROWNING *(Paracelsus)*

251   *Fire*

Men scarcely know how beautiful fire is;
   Each flame of it is as a precious stone
Dissolved in ever-moving light, and *this*
   Belongs to each and all who gaze upon.

PERCY BYSSHE SHELLEY
(The Witch of Atlas)

252   *In a Deep Cave*

One faint eternal eventide of gems.

JOHN KEATS *(Endymion,* II)

253   *The Sea*

And her far seas moan as a single shell.

DANTE GABRIEL ROSSETTI *(Venus)*

254 *Moonlight on the Calm Ocean*

Her beams bemocked the sultry main,
Like April hoar-frost spread;
But where the ship's huge shadow lay,
The charmèd water burnt alway
A still and awful red.

Beyond the shadow of the ship,
I watched the water-snakes:
They moved in tracks of shining white,
And when they reared, the elfish light
Fell off in hoary flakes.

Within the shadow of the ship
I watched their rich attire:
Blue, glossy green, and velvet black,
They coiled and swam; and every track
Was a flash of golden fire.

SAMUEL   TAYLOR   COLERIDGE
(*The Ancient Mariner*)

255   *Fish in Rivers*

The bright-ey'd perch with fins of Tyrian dye,
The silver eel, in shining volumes roll'd,
The yellow carp, in scales bedropp'd with gold,
Swift trouts, diversified with crimson stains,
And pikes, the tyrants of the wat'ry plains.

ALEXANDER   POPE   (*Windsor Forest*)

256 From *The Fish, The Man, and the Spirit*

Man's life is warm, glad, sad, 'twixt loves and graves,
   Boundless in hope, honoured with pangs austere,
Heaven-gazing; and his angel-wings he craves:—
   The fish is swift, small-needing, vague, yet clear,
A cold, sweet, silver life, wrapped in round waves,
   Quickened with touches of transporting fear.

LEIGH   HUNT

257

O Lord! methought what pain it was to drown!
What dreadful noise of water in mine ears!
What sights of ugly death within mine eyes!
Methought I saw a thousand fearful wrecks;

A thousand men that fishes gnaw'd upon;
Wedges of gold, great anchors, heaps of pearl,
Inestimable stones, unvalued jewels,
All scatter'd in the bottom of the sea.
Some lay in dead men's skulls; and in those holes
Where eyes did once inhabit, there were crept,
As 'twere in scorn of eyes, reflecting gems,
That woo'd the slimy bottom of the deep,
And mock'd the dead bones that lay scatter'd by.

WILLIAM SHAKESPEARE

(King Richard III, I, 4)

258 *Magna est Veritas*

Here, in this little Bay,
Full of tumultuous life and great repose,
Where, twice a day,
The purposeless, glad ocean comes and goes,
Under high cliffs, and far from the huge town,
I sit me down.
For want of me the world's course will not fail:
When all its work is done, the lie shall rot;
The truth is great, and shall prevail,
When none cares whether it prevail or not.

COVENTRY PATMORE

259 *On a Greek Island*

It was a wild and breaker-beaten coast,
    With cliffs above, and a broad sandy shore,
Guarded by shoals and rocks as by an host,
    With here and there a creek, whose aspect wore
A better welcome to the tempest-tost;
    And rarely ceased the haughty billow's roar,
Save on the dead long summer days, which make
The outstretch'd ocean glitter like a lake. . . .

It was the cooling hour, just when the rounded
    Red sun sinks down behind the azure hill,
Which then seems as if the whole earth it bounded,
    Circling all nature, hush'd, and dim, and still,

138

With the far mountain-crescent half surrounded
    On one side, and the deep sea calm and chill
Upon the other, and the rosy sky,
With one star sparkling through it like an eye.

And thus they wander'd forth, and hand in hand,
    Over the shining pebbles and the shells,
Glided along the smooth and harden'd sand,
    And in the worn and wild receptacles
Work'd by the storms, yet work'd as it were plann'd
    In hollow halls, with sparry roofs and cells,
They turn'd to rest; and, each clasp'd by an arm,
Yielded to the deep twilight's purple charm.

They look'd up to the sky, whose floating glow
    Spread like a rosy ocean, vast and bright;
They gazed upon the glittering sea below,
    Whence the broad moon rose circling into sight;
They heard the waves splash, and the wind so low,
    And saw each other's dark eyes darting light
Into each other—and, beholding this,
Their lips drew near, and clung into a kiss. . . .

They were alone, but not alone as they
    Who shut in chambers think of loneliness;
The silent ocean, and the starlight bay,
    The twilight glow which momently grew less,
The voiceless sands, and dropping caves, that lay
    Around them, made them to each other press,
As if there were no life beneath the sky
Save theirs, and that their life could never die.

LORD BYRON (*Don Juan*, II)

260   *In the Arctic*

So 'mid the ice of the far northern sea
A star about the arctic circle may
Than ours yield clearer light, yet that but shall
Serve at the frozen pilot's funeral.

WILLIAM HABINGTON
(*Elegy on George Talbot*)

261 *The Eagle*

He clasps the crag with crooked hands;
Close to the sun in lonely lands,
Ring'd with the azure world, he stands.

The wrinkled sea beneath him crawls;
He watches from his mountain walls,
And like a thunderbolt he falls.

ALFRED, LORD TENNYSON

262

Where shall I learn to get my peace again?
To banish thoughts of that most hateful land,
Dungeoner of my friends, that wicked strand
Where they were wreck'd and live a wrecked life;
That monstrous region, whose dull rivers pour,
Ever from their sordid urns unto the shore,
Unown'd of any weedy-hairèd gods;
Whose winds, all zephyrless, hold scourging rods,
Iced in the great lakes, to afflict mankind;
Whose rank-grown forests, frosted, black, and blind,
Would fright a Dryad; whose harsh herbag'd meads
Make lean and lank the starv'd ox while he feeds;
There bad flowers have no scent, birds no sweet song,
And great unerring Nature once seems wrong.

JOHN KEATS *(Lines to Fanny)*

263

Lo! where Maeotis sleeps, and hardly flows
The freezing Tanais through a waste of snows.

ALEXANDER POPE *(The Dunciad)*

264

Doth not a Teneriffe or higher hill
Rise so high like a rock, that one might think
The floating moon would shipwreck there and sink?

JOHN DONNE
(An Anatomy of the World: The First Anniversary)

Cold upon the dead volcano sleeps the gleam of dying day.

ALFRED, LORD TENNYSON
(*Locksley Hall Sixty Years After*)

266   *The River Oxus*

But the majestic river floated on,
Out of the mist and hum of that low land,
Into the frosty starlight, and there mov'd,
Rejoicing, through the hush'd Chorasmian waste,
Under the solitary moon: he flow'd
Right for the Polar Star, past Orgunjè,
Brimming, and bright, and large: then sands begin
To hem his watery march, and dam his streams,
And split his currents; that for many a league
The shorn and parcell'd Oxus strains along
Through beds of sand and matted rushy isles—
Oxus, forgetting the bright speed he had
In his high mountain cradle in Pamere,
A foil'd circuitous wanderer:—till at last
The long'd-for dash of waves is heard, and wide
His luminous home of waters opens, bright
And tranquil, from whose floor the new-bath'd stars
Emerge, and shine upon the Aral Sea.

MATTHEW ARNOLD
(*Sohrab and Rustum*)

267

The sweetness of the Arabian wind still blowing
Upon the treasures of perfumes and spices.

JOHN FLETCHER (*The Bloody Brother*, V, 2)

268   *Silence*

There is a silence where hath been no sound,
  There is a silence where no sound may be,
  In the cold grave—under the deep, deep sea,
Or in wide desert where no life is found,

Which hath been mute, and still must sleep pro-
    found;
  No voice is hush'd—no life treads silently,
  But clouds and cloudy shadows wander free,
That never spoke, over the idle ground:
But in green ruins, in the desolate walls
  Of antique palaces, where Man hath been,
Though the dun fox or wild hyæna calls,
  And owls, that flit continually between,
Shriek to the echo, and the low winds moan—
There the true Silence is, self-conscious and alone.

THOMAS HOOD

269

    There's no virtue in sand:
  It is the rose that makes the wilderness.

CECIL DAY LEWIS (Transitional Poem)

270   From Ruth

He spake of plants that hourly change
Their blossoms, through a boundless range
    Of intermingling hues;
With budding, fading, faded flowers
They stand the wonder of the bowers
    From morn to evening dews.

He told of the magnolia, spread
High as a cloud, high over head!
    The cypress and her spire;
—Of flowers that with one scarlet gleam
Cover a hundred leagues, and seem
    To set the hills on fire. . . .

The wind, the tempest roaring high,
The tumult of a tropic sky
    Might well be dangerous food
For him, a youth to whom was given
So much of earth—so much of heaven,
    And such impetuous blood.

Whatever in those climes he found
Irregular in sight or sound
  Did to his mind impart
A kindred impulse, seem'd allied
To his own powers, and justified
  The workings of his heart.

Nor less, to feed voluptuous thought,
The beauteous forms of Nature wrought,—
  Fair trees and gorgeous flowers;
The breezes their own languor lent;
The stars had feelings, which they sent
  Into those favour'd bowers.

WILLIAM WORDSWORTH

271 *Port of Holy Peter*

The blue laguna rocks and quivers,
  Dull gurgling eddies twist and spin,
The climate does for people's livers,
  It's a nasty place to anchor in
    Is Spanish port,
    Fever port,
    Port of Holy Peter.

The town begins on the sea-beaches,
  And the town's mad with the stinging flies,
The drinking water's mostly leeches,
  It's a far remove from Paradise
    Is Spanish port,
    Fever port,
    Port of Holy Peter.

There's sand-bagging and throat-slitting,
  And quiet graves in the sea slime,
Stabbing, of course, and rum-hitting,
  Dirt, and drink, and stink, and crime,
    In Spanish port,
    Fever port,
    Port of Holy Peter.

All the day the wind's blowing
　　From the sick swamp below the hills,
All the night the plague's growing,
　　And the dawn brings the fever chills,
　　　　In Spanish port,
　　　　Fever port,
　　　　Port of Holy Peter.

You get a thirst there's no slaking,
　　You get the chills and fever-shakes,
Tongue yellow and head aching,
　　And then the sleep that never wakes.
And all the year the heat's baking,
　　The sea rots and the earth quakes,
　　　　In Spanish port,
　　　　Fever port,
　　　　Port of Holy Peter.

JOHN MASEFIELD

272　　　　*By a Lake in Africa*

The naked negress raised on high her arms,
　　Round as palm-saplings; cup-shaped either breast,
Unchecked by needless shames or cold alarms,
　　Swelled, like a burning mountain, with the zest
Of inward life, and tipped itself with fire:
　　Fashioned to crush a lover or a foe,
　　　　Her proud limbs owned their strength, her waist
　　　　its span,
Her fearless form its faultless curves. And lo!—
　　The lion and the serpent and the man
Watched her the while with each his own desire.

ARTHUR O'SHAUGHNESSY (Black Marble)

273　　　　*The Tiger*

Tiger, Tiger, burning bright
In the forests of the night,
What immortal hand or eye
Could frame thy fearful symmetry?

In what distant deeps or skies
Burnt the fire of thine eyes?
On what wings dare he aspire?
What the hand dare seize the fire?

And what shoulder and what art
Could twist the sinews of thy heart?
And when thy heart began to beat,
What dread hand forged thy dread feet?

What the hammer? what the chain?
In what furnace was thy brain?
What the anvil? what dread grasp
Dare its deadly terrors clasp?

When the stars threw down their spears,
And water'd heaven with their tears,
Did He smile His work to see?
Did He who made the Lamb make thee?

Tiger, Tiger, burning bright
In the forests of the night,
What immortal hand or eye
Dare frame thy fearful symmetry?

WILLIAM BLAKE

274   *The Greater Cats*

The greater cats with golden eyes
Stare out between the bars.
Deserts are there, and different skies,
And night with different stars.
They prowl the aromatic hill,
And mate as fiercely as they kill,
And hold the freedom of their will
To roam, to love, to drink their fill;
But this beyond their wit know I:
Man lives a little, and for long shall die.

Their kind across the desert range
Where tulips spring from stones,
Not knowing they will suffer change
Or vultures pick their bones.
Their strength's eternal in their sight,
They rule the terror of the night,
They overtake the deer in flight,
And in their arrogance they smite;
But I am sage, if they are strong:
Man's love is transient as his death is long.

Yet oh what powers to deceive!
My wit is turned to faith,
And at this moment I believe
In love, and scout at death.
I came from nowhere, and shall be
Strong, steadfast, swift, eternally:
I am a lion, a stone, a tree,
And as the Polar star in me
Is fixed my constant heart on thee.
Ah, may I stay forever blind
With lions, tigers, leopards, and their kind.

VICTORIA SACKVILLE-WEST

275   *In the Hindu Kush*

There the voluptuous nightingales,
    Are awake through all the broad noonday.
When one with bliss or sadness fails,
    And through the windless ivy-boughs,
    Sick with sweet love, droops dying away
On its mate's music-panting bosom;
Another from the swinging blossom,
    Watching to catch the languid close
    Of the last strain, then lifts on high
    The wings of the weak melody,
'Till some new strain of feeling bear
    The song, and all the woods are mute;
When there is heard through the dim air

The rush of wings, and rising there
 Like many a lake-surrounded flute,
Sounds overflow the listener's brain
So sweet, that joy is almost pain.

PERCY BYSSHE SHELLEY

(*Prometheus Unbound*, II, 2)

276 *A Song Heard in England*

Perhaps the self-same song that found a path
 Through the sad heart of Ruth, when, sick for home,
  She stood in tears amid the alien corn;
   The same that oft-times hath
 Charm'd magic casements, opening on the foam
 Of perilous seas, in faery lands forlorn.

JOHN KEATS (*Ode to a Nightingale*)

277 *In Paradise*

Now came still evening on, and twilight gray
Had in her sober livery all things clad;
Silence accompanied, for beast and bird,
They to their grassy couch, these to their nests
Were slunk, all but the wakeful nightingale;
She all night long her amorous descant sung;
Silence was pleased.

JOHN MILTON (*Paradise Lost*, IV)

278 *A Dirge*

Call for the robin redbreast and the wren,
Since o'er shady groves they hover,
And with leaves and flowers do cover
The friendless bodies of unburied men.
Call unto his funeral dole
The ant, the field-mouse and the mole,

To rear him hillocks that shall keep him warm,
And (when gay tombs are robbed) sustain no harm.
But keep the wolf far thence, that's foe to men,
For with his nails he'll dig them up again.

JOHN WEBSTER (The White Devil, V, 4)

279

When creatures first were formed,
    They had by Nature's laws
The bulls, their horns; the horses, hoofs;
    The lions, teeth and paws;
To hares she swiftness gave;
    To fishes fins assigned;
To birds, their wings; so no defence
    Was left to womankind.
But, to supply that want,
    She gave her such a face
Which make the bold, the fierce, the swift,
    To stoop and plead for grace.

GEFFREY WHITNEY

280 *April in England*

Yesterday the sullen year
    Saw the snowy whirlwind fly;
Mute was the music of the air,
    The herd stood drooping by;
Their raptures now that wildly flow
No yesterday nor morrow know;
'Tis man alone that joy descries
With forward and reverted eyes. . . .

See the wretch, that long has tossed
    On the thorny bed of pain,
At length repair his vigour lost,
    And breathe and walk again;

The meanest floweret of the vale,
The simplest note that swells the gale,
The common sun, the air, the skies,
To him are opening paradise.

THOMAS GRAY

(Fragment of *Ode on the Pleasure Arising from Vicissitude*)

281   From *Yardley Oak*

Time made thee what thou wast—king of the woods;
And time hath made thee what thou art—a cave
For owls to roost in. Once thy spreading boughs
O'erhung the champaign; and the numerous flock
That graz'd it stood beneath that ample cope
Uncrowded, yet safe shelter'd from the storm.
No flock frequents thee now. Thou hast outliv'd
Thy popularity, and art become
(Unless verse rescue thee awhile) a thing
Forgotten, as the foliage of thy youth.
    While thus through all the stages thou hast push'd
Of treeship—first a seedling hid in grass,
Then twig, then sapling, and, as century roll'd
Slow after century, a giant bulk
Of girth enormous, with moss-cushion'd root
Upheav'd above the soil, and sides emboss'd
With prominent wens globose,—till at the last
The rottenness, which Time is charged to inflict
On other mighty ones, found also thee—
What exhibitions various hath the world
Witness'd of mutability in all
That we account most durable below! . . .
    Time was, when settling on thy leaf, a fly
Could shake thee to the root—and time has been
When tempests could not. . . .
    Thine arms have left thee. Winds have rent them off
Long since, and rovers of the forest wild
With bow and shaft have burnt them. Some have left
A splinter'd stump bleach'd to a snowy white;
And some memorial none where once they grew.

Yet life still lingers in thee, and puts forth
Proof not contemptible of what she can,
Even where death predominates. The spring
Finds thee not less alive to her sweet force
Than yonder upstarts of the neighbouring wood,
So much thy juniors, who their birth receiv'd
Half a millennium since the date of thine.

WILLIAM COWPER

282   From *Ode to Sir Lucius Cary and Sir H. Morison*

It is not growing like a tree
In bulk, doth make man better be;
Or standing long an oak, three hundred year,
To fall a log at last, dry, bald, and sere:
     A lily of a day
     Is fairer far in May,
Although it fall and die that night;
It was the plant and flower of light.
In small proportions we just beauties see;
And in short measures, life may perfect be.

BEN JONSON

283   *To Daffodils*

Fair daffodils, we weep to see
     You haste away so soon:
As yet the early-rising sun
     Has not attain'd his noon.
        Stay, stay
      Until the hasting day
        Has run
      But to the evensong;
And, having pray'd together, we
     Will go with you along.

We have short time to stay, as you,
     We have as short a spring;
As quick a growth to meet decay,
     As you, or anything.

We die
As your hours do, and dry
Away
Like to the summer's rain;
Or as the pearls of morning's dew,
Ne'er to be found again.

ROBERT HERRICK

284 *Spring*

Nothing is so beautiful as spring—
    When weeds, in wheels, shoot long and lovely and lush;
    Thrush's eggs look little low heavens, and thrush
Through the echoing timber does so rinse and wring
The ear, it strikes like lightning to hear him sing;
    The glassy peartree leaves and blooms, they brush
    The descending blue; that blue is all in a rush
With richness; the racing lambs too have fair their fling.

What is all this juice and all this joy?
    A strain of the earth's sweet being in the beginning
In Eden garden.—Have, get, before it cloy,
    Before it cloud, Christ, lord, and sour with sinning,
Innocent mind and Mayday in girl and boy,
    Most, O maid's child, thy choice and worthy the winning.

GERARD MANLEY HOPKINS

285 *Perdita Wishes for Flowers*

O Proserpina,
For the flowers now, that, frighted, thou lett'st fall
From Dis's wagon! daffodils,
That come before the swallow dares, and take
The winds of March with beauty; violets dim,
But sweeter than the lids of Juno's eyes
Or Cytherea's breath; pale primroses,
That die unmarried, ere they can behold

Bright Phoebus in his strength—a malady
Most incident to maids; bold oxlips and
The crown-imperial; lilies of all kinds,
The flower-de-luce being one!

WILLIAM SHAKESPEARE

(*The Winter's Tale*, IV, 3)

286   From *Lycidas*

Bring the rathe primrose that forsaken dies,
The tufted crow-toe, and pale jessamine,
The white pink, and the pansy freaked with jet,
The glowing violet,
The musk-rose, and the well-attired woodbine,
The cowslips wan that hang the pensive head,
And every flower that sad embroidery wears:
Bid Amaranthus all his beauty shed,
And daffadillies fill their cups with tears,
To strew the laureate hearse where Lycid lies.

JOHN MILTON

287   *The Sick Rose*

O Rose, thou art sick!
The invisible worm,
That flies in the night,
In the howling storm,

Has found out thy bed
Of crimson joy;
And his dark secret love
Does thy life destroy.

WILLIAM BLAKE

288   *Bees*

The singing masons building roofs of gold.

WILLIAM SHAKESPEARE

(*King Henry V*, I, 2)

289 *The Snail*

I love at early morn . . .
To note on hedgerow baulks, in moisture sprent,
    The jetty snail creep from the mossy thorn,
With earnest heed, and tremulous intent,
    Frail brother of the morn.

JOHN CLARE (Summer Images)

290

Yet the lark's shrill fife may come
    At the daybreak from the fallow,
And the bittern sound his drum,
    Booming from the sedgy shallow.

SIR WALTER SCOTT
(The Lady of the Lake)

291

Mine is the heron's flight
Which makes a solitude of any sky.

CECIL DAY LEWIS (Transitional Poem)

292 From *Thyrsis*

So, some tempestuous morn in early June,
    When the year's primal burst of bloom is o'er,
        Before the roses and the longest day—
    When garden-walks, and all the grassy floor,
        With blossoms, red and white, of fallen May,
            And chestnut-flowers are strewn—
        So have I heard the cuckoo's parting cry,
            From the wet field, through the vext garden-trees,
            Come with the volleying rain and tossing breeze:
        The bloom is gone and with the bloom go I.

Too quick despairer, wherefore wilt thou go?
  Soon will the high Midsummer pomps come on,
    Soon will the musk carnations break and swell,
  Soon shall we have gold-dusted snapdragon,
    Sweet-William with its homely cottage-smell,
      And stocks in fragrant blow;
  Roses that down the alleys shine afar,
    And open, jasmine-muffled lattices,
    And groups under the dreaming garden-trees,
  And the full moon, and the white evening-star.

MATTHEW ARNOLD

293

Clear had the day been from the dawn,
  All chequer'd was the sky;
Thin clouds, like scarfs of cobweb lawn,
  Veiled heaven's most glorious eye.

The wind had no more strength than this,
  That leisurely it blew,
To make one leaf the next to kiss,
  That closely by it grew.

The rills that on the pebbles played
  Might now be heard at will;
This world they only music made,
  Else everything was still.

The flowers, like brave embroidered girls,
  Looked as they much desired
To see whose head with orient pearls
  Most curiously was tyred.

And to itself the subtle air
  Such sovereignty assumes,
That it receiv'd too large a share
  From Nature's rich perfumes.

MICHAEL DRAYTON

(The Muses' Elizium)

For when thy folding-star arising shows
His paly circlet, at his warning lamp
 The fragrant Hours, and Elves
 Who slept in flowers the day,

And many a Nymph who wreathes her brows with
  sedge
And sheds the fresh'ning dew, and, lovelier still,
 The pensive Pleasures sweet,
 Prepare thy shadowy car:

Then lead, calm vot'ress, where some sheety lake
Cheers the lone heath, or some time-hallowed pile,
 Or upland fallows grey
 Reflect its last cool gleam.

But when chill blust'ring winds, or driving rain,
Forbid my willing feet, be mine the hut
 That, from the mountain's side,
 Views wilds and swelling floods,

And hamlets brown, and dim-discover'd spires,
And hears their simple bell, and marks o'er all
 Thy dewy fingers draw
 The gradual dusky veil.

WILLIAM COLLINS

295 *The Way through the Woods*

They shut the road through the woods
 Seventy years ago.
Weather and rain have undone it again,
 And now you would never know
There was once a path through the woods
 Before they planted the trees.
It is underneath the coppice and heath,
 And the thin anemones.
 Only the keeper sees

That, where the ring-dove broods,
   And the badgers roll at ease,
There was once a road through the woods.

Yet, if you enter the woods
   Of a summer evening late,
When the night-air cools on the trout-ring'd pools
   Where the otter whistles his mate,
(They fear not men in the woods
   Because they see so few)
You will hear the beat of a horse's feet
   And the swish of a skirt in the dew,
   Steadily cantering through
The misty solitudes,
   As though they perfectly knew
The old lost road through the woods . . .
But there is no road through the woods!

RUDYARD KIPLING

296   From *The Garden*

What wond'rous life is this I lead!
Ripe apples drop about my head;
The luscious clusters of the vine
Upon my mouth do crush their wine;
The nectarine and curious peach
Into my hands themselves do reach;
Stumbling on melons, as I pass,
Ensnared with flowers, I fall on grass.

Meanwhile the mind, from pleasure less,
Withdraws into its happiness;—
The mind, that ocean where each kind
Does straight its own resemblance find;—
Yet it creates, transcending these,
Far other worlds, and other seas,
Annihilating all that's made
To a green thought in a green shade.

Here at the fountain's sliding foot,
Or at some fruit-tree's mossy root,

Casting the body's vest aside,
My soul into the boughs does glide:
There, like a bird, it sits and sings,
Then whets and claps its silver wings,
And, till prepar'd for longer flight,
Waves in its plumes the various light.

Such was that happy garden-state,
While man there walked without a mate:
After a place so pure and sweet,
What other help could yet be meet!
But 'twas beyond a mortal's share
To wander solitary there:
Two paradises 'twere in one,
To live in paradise alone.

ANDREW MARVELL

297

Ah! Sun-flower! weary of time,
Who countest the steps of the sun;
Seeking after that sweet golden clime,
Where the traveller's journey is done;

Where the Youth pined away with desire,
And the pale Virgin shrouded in snow,
Arise from their graves, and aspire
Where my Sun-flower wishes to go.

WILLIAM BLAKE

298   *The Osmunda Fern in September*

Lovelier, in its own retired abode
On Grasmere's beach, than Naiad by the side
Of Grecian brook, or Lady of the Mere,
Sole-sitting by the shores of old romance.

WILLIAM WORDSWORTH
('*A Narrow Girdle*')

The green elm with the one great bough of gold
Lets leaves into the grass slip, one by one,—
The short hill grass, the mushrooms small milk-white,
Harebell and scabious and tormentil,
That blackberry and gorse, in dew and sun,
Bow down to; and the wind travels too light
To shake the fallen birch leaves from the fern;
The gossamers wander at their own will.
At heavier steps than birds' the squirrels scold.
The rich scene has grown fresh again and new
As Spring and to the touch is not more cool
Than it is warm to the gaze; and now I might
As happy be as earth is beautiful,
Were I some other or with earth could turn
In alternation of violet and rose,
Harebell and snowdrop, at their season due,
And gorse that has no time not to be gay.
But if this be not happiness,—who knows?
Some day I shall think this a happy day,
And this mood by the name of melancholy
Shall no more blackened and obscured be.

EDWARD THOMAS

Season of mists and mellow fruitfulness!
  Close bosom-friend of the maturing sun;
Conspiring with him how to load and bless
  With fruit the vines that round the thatch-eaves run;
To bend with apples the moss'd cottage-trees,
  And fill all fruit with ripeness to the core;
    To swell the gourd, and plump the hazel shells
  With a sweet kernel; to set budding more
And still more, later flowers for the bees,
Until they think warm days will never cease,
  For summer has o'er-brimm'd their clammy cells.

Who hath not seen thee oft amid thy store?
　　Sometimes whoever seeks abroad may find
Thee sitting careless on a granary floor,
　　Thy hair soft-lifted by the winnowing wind;
Or on a half-reap'd furrow sound asleep,
　　Drowsed with the fume of poppies, while thy hook
　　　　Spares the next swath and all its twinèd flowers;
　　And sometimes like a gleaner thou dost keep
Steady thy laden head across a brook;
Or by a cider-press, with patient look,
　　Thou watchest the last oozings, hours by hours.

Where are the songs of Spring? Aye, where are they?
　　Think not of them,—thou hast thy music too,
While barrèd clouds bloom the soft-dying day
　　And touch the stubble-plains with rosy hue;
Then in a wailful choir the small gnats mourn
　　Among the river-sallows, borne aloft
　　　　Or sinking as the light wind lives or dies;
　　And full-grown lambs loud bleat from hilly bourn;
Hedge-crickets sing, and now with treble soft
The redbreast whistles from a garden-croft;
　　And gathering swallows twitter in the skies.

JOHN KEATS

301　*To Meadows*

Ye have been fresh and green,
　　Ye have been fill'd with flowers,
And ye the walks have been
　　Where maids have spent their hours.

You have beheld how they
　　With wicker arks did come
To kiss and bear away
　　The richer cowslips home.

You've heard them sweetly sing,
　　And seen them in a round:
Each virgin like a spring,
　　With honeysuckles crown'd.

But now we see none here
   Whose silv'ry feet did tread
And with dishevell'd hair
   Adorn'd this smoother mead.

Like unthrifts, having spent
   Your stock and needy grown,
You're left here to lament
   Your poor estates, alone.

ROBERT HERRICK

302

A widow bird sate mourning for her love
   Upon a wintry bough;
The frozen wind crept on above,
   The freezing stream below.

There was no leaf upon the forest bare,
   No flower upon the ground,
And little motion in the air
   Except the mill-wheel's sound.

PERCY BYSSHE SHELLEY

303   *At Thirty Years of Age*

No more—no more—Oh! never more on me
   The freshness of the heart can fall like dew,
Which out of all the lovely things we see
   Extracts emotions beautiful and new,
Hived in our bosoms like the bag o' the bee.
   Think'st thou the honey with those objects grew?
Alas! 'twas not in them, but in thy power
To double even the sweetness of a flower.

LORD BYRON (Don Juan, I)

A grief without a pang, void, dark, and drear,
   A stifled, drowsy, unimpassioned grief,
   Which finds no natural outlet, no relief,
     In word, or sigh, or tear—
O Lady! in this wan and heartless mood,
To other thoughts by yonder throstle woo'd,
   All this long eve, so balmy and serene,
Have I been gazing on the western sky,
   And its peculiar tint of yellow green:
And still I gaze—and with how blank an eye!
And those thin clouds above, in flakes and bars,
That give away their motion to the stars;
Those stars, that glide behind them or between,
Now sparkling, now bedimmed, but always seen:
Yon crescent Moon, as fixed as if it grew
In its own cloudless, starless lake of blue;
I see them all so excellently fair,
I see, not feel, how beautiful they are!

    My genial spirits fail;
    And what can these avail
To lift the smothering weight from off my breast?
    It were a vain endeavour,
    Though I should gaze for ever
On that green light that lingers in the west:
I may not hope from outward forms to win
The passion and the life, whose fountains are within.

O Lady! we receive but what we give,
And in our life alone does Nature live:
Ours is her wedding-garment, ours her shroud!
   And would we aught behold, of higher worth,
Than that inanimate cold world allowed
To the poor loveless, ever-anxious crowd,
   Ah! from the soul itself must issue forth

A light, a glory, a fair luminous cloud
　　Enveloping the Earth—
And from the soul itself must there be sent
　　A sweet and potent voice, of its own birth,
Of all sweet sounds the life and element!

SAMUEL TAYLOR COLERIDGE

(*Dejection: An Ode*)

305　　*God's Grandeur*

The world is charged with the grandeur of God.
　　It will flame out, like shining from shook foil;
　　It gathers to a greatness, like the ooze of oil
Crushed. Why do men then now not reck his rod?
Generations have trod, have trod, have trod;
　　And all is seared with trade; bleared, smeared with
　　　toil;
　　And wears man's smudge and shares man's smell: the
　　　soil
Is bare now, nor can foot feel, being shod.

And for all this, nature is never spent;
　　There lives the dearest freshness deep down things;
And though the last lights off the black West went,
　　Oh, morning, at the brown brink eastward, springs—
Because the Holy Ghost over the bent
　　World broods with warm breast and with ah! bright
　　　wings.

GERARD MANLEY HOPKINS

306　　From *The Secret Wood*

I only know
Though all men of earth's beauty speak
Beauty here I do not seek
More than I sought it on my mother's cheek.

ANDREW YOUNG

Brook and road
Were fellow-travellers in this gloomy Pass,
And with them did we journey several hours
At a slow step. The immeasurable height
Of woods decaying, never to be decayed,
The stationary blasts of waterfalls,
And in the narrow rent, at every turn,
Winds thwarting winds bewildered and forlorn,
The torrents shooting from the clear blue sky,
The rocks that muttered close upon our ears,
Black drizzling crags that spake by the wayside
As if a voice were in them, the sick sight
And giddy prospect of the raving stream,
The unfettered clouds and regions of the heavens,
Tumult and peace, the darkness and the light—
Were all like workings of one mind, the features
Of the same face, blossoms upon one tree,
Characters of the great Apocalypse,
The types and symbols of Eternity,
Of first, and last, and midst, and without end.

WILLIAM WORDSWORTH

308 *To an Independent Preacher*

Who preached that we should be 'in harmony with Nature'

'In harmony with Nature'? Restless fool,
Who with such heat dost preach what were to thee,
When true, the last impossibility;
To be like Nature strong, like Nature cool:—
Know, man hath all which Nature hath, but more,
And in that *more* lie all his hopes of good.
Nature is cruel; man is sick of blood:
Nature is stubborn; man would fain adore:
Nature is fickle; man hath need of rest:
Nature forgives no debt, and fears no grave:
Man would be mild, and with safe conscience blest.

Man must begin, know this, where Nature ends;
Nature and man can never be fast friends.
Fool, if thou canst not pass her, rest her slave!

MATTHEW ARNOLD

309   *When the World is Burning*

When the world is burning,
Fired within, yet turning
    Round with face unscathed;
Ere fierce flames, uprushing
O'er all lands leap, crushing,
    Till earth fall, fire-swathed;
Up amidst the meadows,
Gently through the shadows,
    Gentle flames will glide,
Small, and blue, and golden.
Though by bard beholden,
When in calm dreams folden,—
    Calm his dreams will bide.

Where the dance is sweeping,
Through the greensward peeping,
    Shall the soft lights start;
Laughing maids, unstaying,
Deeming it trick-playing,
High their robes upswaying,
    O'er the lights shall dart;
And the woodland haunter
Shall not cease to saunter
    When, far down some glade,
Of the great world's burning,
One soft flame upturning
Seems, to his discerning,
    Crocus in the shade.

EBENEZER JONES

I had a dream, which was not all a dream.
The bright sun was extinguish'd, and the stars
Did wander darkling in the eternal space,
Rayless, and pathless, and the icy earth
Swung blind and blackening in the moonless air;
Morn came and went—and came, and brought no day,
And men forgot their passions in the dread
Of this their desolation; and all hearts
Were chilled into a selfish prayer for light . . .
Happy were those who dwelt within the eye
Of the volcanoes, and their mountain-torch:
A fearful hope was all the world contain'd;
Forests were set on fire—but hour by hour
They fell and faded—and the crackling trunks
Extinguish'd with a crash—and all was black. . . .
And War, which for a moment was no more,
Did glut himself again:—a meal was bought
With blood, and each sate sullenly apart
Gorging himself in gloom: no love was left;
All earth was but one thought—and that was death
Immediate and inglorious . . .
                    The world was void,
The populous and the powerful was a lump
Seasonless, herbless, treeless, manless, lifeless—
A lump of death—a chaos of hard clay.
The rivers, lakes, and ocean all stood still,
And nothing stirr'd within their silent depths;
Ships sailorless lay rotting on the sea,
And their masts fell down piecemeal: as they dropp'd
They slept on the abyss without a surge—
The waves were dead; the tides were in their grave,
The moon, their mistress, had expired before;
The winds were wither'd in the stagnant air,
And the clouds perish'd; Darkness had no need
Of aid from them—She was the Universe.

                                        LORD BYRON

Though earth and man were gone,
And suns and universes ceased to be,
  And Thou wert left alone,
Every existence would exist in Thee.

EMILY JANE BRONTË

(*'No coward soul is mine'*)

Be cheerful, sir:
Our revels now are ended. These our actors,
As I foretold you, were all spirits and
Are melted into air, into thin air:
And, like the baseless fabric of this vision,
The cloud-capp'd towers, the gorgeous palaces,
The solemn temples, the great globe itself,
Yea, all which it inherit, shall dissolve
And, like this insubstantial pageant faded,
Leave not a rack behind. We are such stuff
As dreams are made on, and our little life
Is rounded with a sleep.

WILLIAM SHAKESPEARE

(*The Tempest*, IV, 1)

6

THE SPAN OF LIFE

The section deals with the various stages of life from infancy to old age and death, and contains poems on family relationships, other than the relationship between husband and wife which is included in the section *Love*. . . . In this anthology there is no separate section on death. Since men and women may meet death in the course of action, or at a time when they intensely love or are loved, or in the service of a social cause, there are poems which mention death in *Action*, *Love*, and *Man and Society*, and indeed in all sections; nor would the scope of the sections be complete without such poems. Verse on immortality as a religious belief is included in *Man and God*. *The Span of Life* contains poems on death as it may intervene at any stage to curtail or conclude the human span.

---

313   From *Essay on Man*

Behold the child, by Nature's kindly law,
Pleas'd with a rattle, tickled with a straw:
Some livelier plaything gives his youth delight,
A little louder, but as empty quite:
Scarfs, garters, gold, amuse his riper stage,
And beads and prayer-books are the toys of age:
Pleas'd with this bauble still, as that before;
Till tir'd he sleeps, and Life's poor play is o'er.

ALEXANDER POPE

314

On parent knees, a naked new-born child,
Weeping thou sat'st, when all around thee smiled:
So live, that, sinking in thy last long sleep,
Calm thou may'st smile, while all around thee weep.

SIR WILLIAM JONES
(*After the Persian*)

315 *A Cradle Song*

Sleep! sleep! beauty bright,
Dreaming o'er the joys of night:
Sleep! Sleep! in thy sleep
Little sorrows sit and weep.

Sweet babe, in thy face
Soft desires I can trace,
Secret joys and secret smiles,
Little pretty infant wiles.

As thy softest limbs I feel,
Smiles as of the morning steal
O'er thy cheek, and o'er thy breast
Where thy little heart does rest.

O, the cunning wiles that creep
In thy little heart asleep!
When thy little heart does wake,
Then the dreadful lightnings break.

WILLIAM BLAKE

316 From *Childhood*

I cannot reach it; and my striving eye
Dazzles at it, as at eternity.
Were now that chronicle alive,
Those white designs which children drive,
And the thoughts of each harmless hour,
With their content too in my pow'r,
Quickly would I make my path ev'n,
And by mere playing go to heaven.

HENRY VAUGHAN

317 *A Boy's Song*

Where the pools are bright and deep,
Where the grey trout lies asleep,
Up the river and over the lea,
That's the way for Billy and me.

Where the blackbird sings the latest,
Where the hawthorn blooms the sweetest,
Where the nestlings chirp and flee,
That's the way for Billy and me.

Where the mowers mow the cleanest,
Where the hay lies thick and greenest,
There to track the homeward bee,
That's the way for Billy and me.

Where the hazel bank is steepest,
Where the shadow falls the deepest,
Where the clustering nuts fall free,
That's the way for Billy and me. . . .

JAMES HOGG

318   *Polixenes and Leontes*

Two lads that thought there was no more behind
But such a day to-morrow as to-day,
And to be boy eternal.

WILLIAM SHAKESPEARE
(*The Winter's Tale*, I, 2)

319   From *Fern Hill*

And honoured among foxes and pheasants by the gay house
Under the new made clouds and happy as the heart was
    long,
      In the sun born over and over,
        I ran my heedless ways,
     My wishes raced through the house high hay
And nothing I cared, at my sky blue trades, that time allows
In all his tuneful turning so few and such morning songs
      Before the children green and golden
        Follow him out of grace.

Nothing I cared, in the lamb white days, that time would
    take me
Up to the swallow thronged loft by the shadow of my hand,
      In the moon that is always rising,
          Nor that riding to sleep
      I should hear him fly with the high fields
And wake to the farm forever fled from the childless land.
Oh as I was young and easy in the mercy of his means,
        Time held me green and dying
      Though I sang in my chains like the sea.

DYLAN THOMAS

320   *Spring and Fall; To a Young Child*

    Márgarét, are you gríeving
    Over Goldengrove unleaving?
    Leáves, líke the things of man, you
    With your fresh thoughts care for, can you?
    Ah! ás the heart grows older
    It will come to such sights colder
    By and by, nor spare a sigh
    Though worlds of wanwood leafmeal lie;
    And yet you wíll weep and know why.
    Now no matter, child, the name:
    Sórrow's spríngs áre the same.
    Nor mouth had, no nor mind, expressed
    What heart heard of, ghost guessed:
    It ís the blight man was born for,
    It is Margaret you mourn for.

GERARD MANLEY HOPKINS

321   *After the Death of Giovanni's Mother*

Giovanni: What do the dead do, uncle? do they eat,
    Hear music, go a-hunting, and be merry,
    As we that live?
Francisco: No, coz, they sleep.
Giovanni: Lord, Lord, that I were dead!
    I have not slept these six nights.—When do they
    wake?

Francisco: When God shall please.

Giovanni: Good God, let her sleep ever!
For I have known her wake an hundred nights,
When all the pillow where she laid her head
Was brine-wet with her tears. I am to complain to
      you, sir;
I'll tell you how they have used her now she's
      dead:
They wrapped her in a cruel fold of lead,
And would not let me kiss her.

Francisco: Thou didst love her.

Giovanni: I have often heard her say she gave me suck,
And it should seem by that she dearly loved me,
Since princes seldom do it.

Francisco: O, all of my poor sister that remains.—
Take him away, for God's sake!

JOHN WEBSTER

(*The White Devil*, III, 1)

322   From *On My First Son*

Rest in soft peace: and, asked, say 'Here doth lie
Ben Jonson his best piece of poetry.'

BEN JONSON

323   *Maternity*

One wept whose only child was dead,
New-born, ten years ago.
'Weep not; he is in bliss,' they said.
She answered, 'Even so.

'Ten years ago was born in pain
A child, not now forlorn.
But oh, ten years ago, in vain,
A mother, a mother was born.'

ALICE MEYNELL

324 Leidenberch, about to Commit Suicide, Has Said Good-night to His Son

How nature rises now and turns me woman
When I should most be man! Sweet heart, farewell,
Farewell for ever. When we get us children,
We then do give our freedoms up to fortune
And lose that native courage we are born to.
To die were nothing,—simply to leave the light;
No more than going to our beds and sleeping;
But to leave all these dearnesses behind us,
These figures of ourselves that we call blessings,
Is that which troubles. Can man beget a thing
That shall be dearer than himself unto him?

JOHN FLETCHER and PHILIP MASSINGER
(*Barnavelt*, III, 6)

325

In ancient shadows and twilights
Where childhood had strayed,
The world's great sorrows were born
And its heroes were made.
In the lost boyhood of Judas
Christ was betrayed.

GEORGE WILLIAM RUSSELL (Æ)
(*Germinal*)

326 *Animula*

'Issues from the hand of God, the simple soul'
To a flat world of changing lights and noise,
To light, dark, dry or damp, chilly or warm;
Moving between the legs of tables and of chairs,
Rising or falling, grasping at kisses and toys,
Advancing boldly, sudden to take alarm,
Retreating to the corner of arm and knee,
Eager to be reassured, taking pleasure

In the fragrant brilliance of the Christmas tree,
Pleasure in the wind, the sunlight and the sea;
Studies the sunlit pattern on the floor
And running stags around a silver tray;
Confounds the actual and the fanciful,
Content with playing-cards and kings and queens,
What the fairies do and what the servants say.
The heavy burden of the growing soul
Perplexes and offends more, day by day;
Week by week, offends and perplexes more
With the imperatives of 'is and seems'
And may and may not, desire and control.
The pain of living and the drug of dreams
Curl up the small soul in the window seat
Behind the *Encyclopaedia Britannica.*
Issues from the hand of time the simple soul
Irresolute and selfish, misshapen, lame,
Unable to fare forward or retreat,
Fearing the warm reality, the offered good,
Denying the importunity of the blood,
Shadow of its own shadows, spectre in its own gloom,
Leaving disordered papers in a dusty room;
Living first in the silence after the viaticum.

Pray for Guiterriez, avid of speed and power,
For Boudin, blown to pieces,
For this one who made a great fortune,
And that one who went his own way.
Pray for Floret, by the boarhound slain between the
    yew trees,
Pray for us now and at the hour of our birth.

                        THOMAS STEARNS ELIOT

327

Ah, Chloris! that I now could sit
    As unconcern'd as when
Your infant beauty could beget
    No pleasure, nor no pain.

When I the dawn used to admire,
   And praised the coming day,
I little thought the growing fire
   Must take my rest away.

Your charms in harmless childhood lay,
   Like metals in the mine:
Age from no face took more away
   Than youth concealed in thine. . . .

SIR CHARLES SEDLEY

328 From *Corinna's Going a-Maying*

Rise, and put on your foliage. . . .

Come, let us go, while we are in our prime,
And take the harmless folly of the time!
   We shall grow old apace, and die
   Before we know our liberty.
   Our life is short, and our days run
   As fast away as does the sun.
And as a vapour or a drop of rain,
Once lost, can ne'er be found again,
   So when or you or I are made
   A fable, song, or fleeting shade,
   All love, all liking, all delight
   Lies drown'd with us in endless night.
Then while time serves, and we are but decaying,
Come, my Corinna, come, let's go a-Maying.

ROBERT HERRICK

329   *Time*

What eye with clear account remarks
   The ebbing of his glass,
When all its sands are diamond sparks,
   That dazzle as they pass?

Ah, who to sober measurement
    Time's happy swiftness brings,
When birds of Paradise have lent
    Their plumage for his wings?

WILLIAM ROBERT SPENCER
(*To the Lady Anne Hamilton*)

330   *The Scholars*

Bald heads forgetful of their sins,
Old, learned, respectable bald heads
Edit and annotate the lines
That young men, tossing on their beds,
Rhymed out in love's despair
To flatter beauty's ignorant ear.

All shuffle there; all cough in ink;
All wear the carpet with their shoes;
All think what other people think;
All know the man their neighbour knows.
Lord, what would they say
Did their Catullus walk that way?

WILLIAM BUTLER YEATS

331   From *The Careless Gallant*

Let us drink and be merry, dance, joke and rejoice,
With claret and sherry, theorbo and voice,
The changeable world to our joy is unjust,
All treasure's uncertain, then down with your dust;
In frolics dispose your pounds, shillings, and pence,
For we shall be nothing a hundred years hence. . . .

Your beautiful bit who hath all eyes upon her,
That her honesty sells for a hogo of honour,
Whose lightness and brightness doth cast such a splendour,
That none are thought fit but the stars to attend her,
Though now she seems pleasant and sweet to the sense,
Will be damnable mouldy a hundred years hence. . . .

Then why should we turmoil in cares and in fears,
Turn all our tranquill'ty to sighs and to tears?
Let's eat, drink and play ere the worms do corrupt us,
For I say that, *Post mortem nulla voluptas*,
For health, wealth and beauty, wit, learning and sense,
Must all come to nothing a hundred years hence.

THOMAS JORDAN

332   *In Time of Plague* (*1593*)

Adieu, farewell earth's bliss,
This world uncertain is;
Fond are life's lustful joys,
Death proves them all but toys.
None from his darts can fly:
I am sick, I must die.
    Lord have mercy on us! . . .

Beauty is but a flower,
Which wrinkles will devour:
Brightness falls from the air;
Queens have died young and fair;
Dust hath closed Helen's eye:
I am sick, I must die.
    Lord have mercy on us!

Strength stoops unto the grave:
Worms feed on Hector brave;
Swords may not fight with fate:
Earth still holds ope her gate.
Come! come! the bells do cry.
I am sick, I must die.
    Lord have mercy on us!

THOMAS NASHE
(*Summer's Last Will and Testament*)

She, whose fair body no such prison was,
But that a soul might well be pleased to pass
An age in her ; she, whose rich beauty lent
Mintage to other beauties, for they went
But for so much as they were like to her ;
She, in whose body—if we dare prefer
This low world to so high a mark as she—
The western treasure, eastern spicery,
Europe, and Afric, and the unknown rest
Were easily found, or what in them was best. . . .
She, of whose soul, if we may say, 'twas gold,
Her body was the electrum, and did hold
Many degrees of that; we understood
Her by her sight; her pure and eloquent blood
Spoke in her cheeks, and so distinctly wrought
That one might almost say, her body thought;
She, she thus richly and largely housed, is gone;
And chides us slow-paced snails who crawl upon
Our prison's prison, earth, nor think us well,
Longer than whilst we bear our brittle shell.

JOHN DONNE
(*An Anatomy of the World: The Second Anniversary*)

334   *Rose Aylmer*

Ah, what avails the sceptred race !
   Ah, what the form divine !
What every virtue, every grace !
   Rose Aylmer, all were thine.

Rose Aylmer, whom these wakeful eyes
   May weep, but never see,
A night of memories and sighs
   I consecrate to thee.

WALTER SAVAGE LANDOR

335 *Dirce*

Stand close around, ye Stygian set,
   With Dirce in one boat convey'd!
Or Charon, seeing, may forget
   That he is old and she a shade.

WALTER SAVAGE LANDOR

336 *Dirge for Fidele*

Fear no more the heat o' the sun,
   Nor the furious winter's rages;
Thou thy worldly task hast done,
   Home art gone, and ta'en thy wages:
Golden lads and girls all must,
As chimney-sweepers, come to dust.

Fear no more the frown o' the great,
   Thou art past the tyrant's stroke;
Care no more to clothe and eat;
   To thee the reed is as the oak:
The sceptre, learning, physic, must
All follow this, and come to dust.

Fear no more the lightning-flash,
   Nor the all-dreaded thunder-stone;
Fear not slander, censure rash;
   Thou hast finish'd joy and moan:
All lovers young, all lovers must
Consign to thee, and come to dust.

WILLIAM SHAKESPEARE

(Cymbeline)

337 'Thou Dost Not Know What 'tis to Die'

Yes, I do know, my lord:
'Tis less than to be born; a lasting sleep;
A quiet resting from all jealousy;
A thing we all pursue; I know besides,

178

It is but giving over of a game
That must be lost.

FRANCIS BEAUMONT and JOHN FLETCHER
(*Philaster*, III, 1)

338   *Epitaph*

Here dead lie we because we did not choose
   To live and shame the land from which we sprung.
Life, to be sure, is nothing much to lose;
   But young men think it is, and we were young.

ALFRED EDWARD HOUSMAN

339   *Lines Written at Twenty-Seven on the Night before Execution for Treason*

The spring is past, and yet it hath not sprung;
   The fruit is dead, and yet the leaves are green;
My youth is gone, and yet I am but young;
   I saw the world, and yet I was not seen;
My thread is cut, and yet it is not spun;
And now I live, and now my life is done.

CHIDIOCK TICHBORNE
('*My Prime of Youth*')

340   From *Don Juan*

My days of love are over; me no more
   The charms of maid, wife, and still less of widow,
Can make the fool of which they made before,—
   In short, I must not lead the life I did do;
The credulous hope of mutual minds is o'er,
   The copious use of claret is forbid too,
So for a good old-gentlemanly vice.
I think I must take up with avarice.

Ambition was my idol, which was broken
  Before the shrines of Sorrow, and of Pleasure;
And the two last have left me many a token,
  O'er which reflection may be made at leisure:
Now, like Friar Bacon's brazen head, I've spoken,
  'Time is, Time was, Time's past';—a chymic
      treasure
Is glittering youth, which I have spent betimes—
My heart in passion, and my head on rhymes.

LORD BYRON (Don Juan, I, 1)

341

The wan moon is settin' behind the white wave,
  And Time is settin' wi' me, o'.

ROBERT BURNS ('Oh, open the Door')

342   From *Ode on Intimations of Immortality*

What though the radiance which was once so bright
Be now for ever taken from my sight,
  Though nothing can bring back the hour
Of splendour in the grass, of glory in the flower;
    We will grieve not, rather find
    Strength in what remains behind;
    In the primal sympathy
    Which having been must ever be;
    In the soothing thoughts that spring
    Out of human suffering;
    In the faith that looks through death,
In years that bring the philosophic mind.

.   .   .   .

I love the brooks which down their channels fret,
Even more than when I tripped lightly as they;
The innocent brightness of a new-born day
        Is lovely yet;

The clouds that gather round the setting sun
Do take a sober colouring from an eye
That hath kept watch o'er man's mortality;
Another race hath been, and other palms are won.
Thanks to the human heart by which we live,
Thanks to its tenderness, its joys, and fears,
To me the meanest flower that blows can give
Thoughts that do often lie too deep for tears.

WILLIAM WORDSWORTH

343

At thirty man suspects himself a fool;
Knows it at forty, and reforms his plan;
At fifty chides his infamous delay,
Pushes his prudent purpose to resolve;
In all the magnanimity of thought
Resolves; and re-resolves; then dies the same.

EDWARD YOUNG (Night Thoughts)

344

When I consider life, 'tis all a cheat;
Yet, fooled with hope, men favour the deceit;
Trust on, and think to-morrow will repay:
To-morrow's falser than the former day;
Lies worse; and while it says, we shall be blest
With some new joys, cuts off what we possessed.
Strange cozenage! None would live past years again,
Yet all hope pleasure in what yet remain;
And, from the dregs of life, think to receive
What the first sprightly running could not give.

JOHN DRYDEN (Aurengzebe, IV, 1)

345

Thou by thy dial's shady stealth mayst know
Time's thievish progress to eternity.

WILLIAM SHAKESPEARE (Sonnet 77)

O World! O Life! O Time!
On whose last steps I climb,
    Trembling at that where I had stood before;
When will return the glory of your prime?
        No more—Oh, never more!

Out of the day and night
A joy has taken flight:
    Fresh spring, and summer, and winter hoar
Move my faint heart with grief, but with delight
        No more—Oh, never more!

PERCY BYSSHE SHELLEY

347   From *The Garden of Proserpine*

From too much love of living.
    From hope and fear set free
We thank with brief thanksgiving
    Whatever gods may be
That no life lives for ever;
That dead men rise up never;
That even the weariest river
    Winds somewhere safe to sea.

Then star nor sun shall waken,
    Nor any change of light:
Nor sound of waters shaken,
    Nor any sound or sight:
Nor wintry leaves nor vernal,
Nor days nor things diurnal;
Only the sleep eternal
    In an eternal night.

ALGERNON CHARLES SWINBURNE

348   *In the Morgue in Paris*

First came the silent gazers; next,
    A screen of glass we're thankful for;
Last, the sight's self, the sermon's text,
    The three men who did most abhor

Their life in Paris yesterday,
   So killed themselves: and now, enthroned
Each on his copper couch, they lay
   Fronting me, waiting to be owned.

      ROBERT BROWNING (*Apparent Failure*)

349

But, Lord Christ, when that it remembreth me
Upon my youth, and on my jollity,
It tickleth me about my hertë root.
Unto this day it doth my hertë boot
That I have had my world as in my time.

      GEOFFREY CHAUCER
        (*The Wife of Bath's Prologue*)

350

Enjoy the present smiling hour,
   And put it out of Fortune's power. . . .
Happy the man, and happy he alone,
   He, who can call to-day his own:
   He, who secure within, can say,
To-morrow do thy worst, for I have lived to-day.
   Be fair, or foul, or rain, or shine,
The joys I have possessed, in spite of fate, are mine.
   Not Heaven itself upon the past has power;
But what has been, has been, and I have had my
     hour.

      JOHN DRYDEN (after HORACE)

351

Each year bears something from us as it flies,
We only blow it farther with our sighs.

      WALTER SAVAGE LANDOR

Though the day of my destiny's over,
    And the star of my fate hath declined,
Thy soft heart refused to discover
    The faults which so many could find;
Though thy soul with my grief was acquainted,
    It shrunk not to share it with me,
And the love which my spirit hath painted
    It never hath found but in *thee*. . . .

Though human, thou didst not deceive me,
    Though woman, thou didst not forsake,
Though loved, thou forborest to grieve me,
    Though slandered, thou never couldst shake;
Though trusted, thou didst not disclaim me,
    Though parted, it was not to fly,
Though watchful, 'twas not to defame me,
    Nor, mute, that the world might belie. . . .

From the wreck of the past, which hath perish'd,
    Thus much I at least may recall,
It hath taught me that what I most cherish'd
    Deserved to be dearest of all:
In the desert a fountain is springing,
    In the wide waste there still is a tree,
And a bird in the solitude singing,
    Which speaks to my spirit of *thee*.

               LORD BYRON   *(Stanzas to Augusta)*

353   *On His Mother*

Me, let the tender office long engage,
To rock the cradle of reposing age,
With lenient arts extend a mother's breath,
Make languor smile, and smooth the bed of death,
Explore the thought, explain the asking eye,
And keep a while one parent from the sky!

             ALEXANDER POPE
               (Epistle to Arbuthnot)

Where art thou, my belovèd son,
Where art thou, worse to me than dead?
Oh, find me, prosperous or undone!
Or, if the grave be now thy bed,
Why am I ignorant of the same,
That I may rest; and neither blame
Nor sorrow may attend thy name? . . .

Ah, little doth the young one dream,
When full of play and childish cares,
What power is in his wildest scream,
Heard by his mother unawares!
He knows it not, he cannot guess;
Years to a mother bring distress,
But do not make her love the less. . . .

Perhaps some dungeon hears thee groan,
Maimed, mangled by inhuman men;
Or thou upon a desert thrown
Inheritest the lion's den;
Or hast been summoned to the deep,
Thou, thou and all thy mates, to keep
An incommunicable sleep.

I look for ghosts, but none will force
Their way to me; 'tis falsely said
That there was ever intercourse
Betwixt the living and the dead;
For, surely, then I should have sight
Of him I wait for day and night,
With love and longings infinite.

My apprehensions come in crowds;
I dread the rustling of the grass;
The very shadows of the clouds
Have power to shake me as they pass:
I question things, and do not find
One that will answer to my mind;
And all the world appears unkind.

Beyond participation lie
My troubles, and beyond relief:
If any chance to heave a sigh,
They pity me, and not my grief.
Then come to me, my son, or send
Some tidings that my woes may end;
I have no other earthly friend.

WILLIAM WORDSWORTH
(*The Affliction of Margaret*)

355

That time of year thou mayst in me behold
  When yellow leaves, or none, or few, do hang
Upon those boughs which shake against the cold,
  Bare ruined choirs, where late the sweet birds sang.

WILLIAM SHAKESPEARE (*Sonnet* 73)

356

No spring nor summer beauty hath such grace
As I have seen in one autumnal face.

JOHN DONNE (*Elegy* IX)

357   From *A Portrait*

Old: yet unchanged;—still pottering in his thoughts;
Still eagerly enslaved by books and print;
Less plagued, perhaps, by rigid musts and oughts,
But no less frantic in vain argument;

Still happy as a child, with its small toys,
Over his inkpot and his bits and pieces,—
Life's arduous, fragile and ingenuous joys,
Whose charm failed never—nay, it even increases! . . .

Haunted by questions no man answered yet;
Pining to leap from A clean on to Z;
Absorbed by problems which the wise forget;
Avid for fantasy—yet how staid a head! . . .

Not yet inert, but with a tortured breast
At hint of that bleak gulf—his last farewell;
Pining for peace, assurance, pause and rest,
Yet slave to what he loves past words to tell;

A foolish, fond old man, his bed-time nigh,
Who still at western window stays to win
A transient respite from the latening sky,
And scarce can bear it when the sun goes in.

WALTER DE LA MARE

358   *After Long Silence*

Speech after long silence; it is right,
All other lovers being estranged or dead,
Unfriendly lamplight hid under its shade,
The curtains drawn upon unfriendly night,
That we descant and yet again descant
Upon the supreme theme of Art and Song:
Bodily decrepitude is wisdom; young
We loved each other and were ignorant.

WILLIAM BUTLER YEATS

359   *The End of Man's Life*

Then Old Age and Experience, hand in hand,
Lead him to Death, and make him understand,
After a search so painful, and so long,
That all his life he has been in the wrong.
Huddled in dirt the reasoning engine lies,
Who was so proud, so witty, and so wise.

JOHN WILMOT, EARL OF ROCHESTER
(A Satire Against Mankind)

Through many days they toil; then comes a day
They die not,—never having lived,—but cease.

DANTE GABRIEL ROSSETTI

(*The House of Life*)

361 *On the Death of an Epicure*

At length, my friends, the feast of life is o'er;
I've eat sufficient—and I'll drink no more:
My night is come; I've spent a jovial day;
'Tis time to part: but oh! what is to pay?

RICHARD GRAVES

362

I strove with none, for none was worth my strife:
   Nature I loved, and next to Nature, Art:
I warmed both hands before the fire of Life;
   It sinks; and I am ready to depart.

WALTER SAVAGE LANDOR

363

What, in ill thoughts again? Men must endure
Their going hence, even as their coming hither:
Ripeness is all.

WILLIAM SHAKESPEARE

(*King Lear*, V, 2)

364

We cease to grieve, cease to be fortune's slaves,
Nay, cease to die, by dying.

JOHN WEBSTER

(*The White Devil*, V, 6)

365   Death

Nor dread nor hope attend
A dying animal;
A man awaits his end
Dreading and hoping all;
Many times he died,
Many times rose again.
A great man in his pride
Confronting murderous men
Casts derision upon
Supersession of breath;
He knows death to the bone—
Man has created death.

WILLIAM BUTLER YEATS

366   The Death of Antony

O, withered is the garland of the war,
The soldier's pole is fallen: young men and girls
Are equal now with men: the odds is gone,
And there is nothing left remarkable
Beneath the visiting moon.

WILLIAM SHAKESPEARE
(*Antony and Cleopatra*, IV, 13)

367

Death, in itself, is nothing; but we fear
To be we know not what, we know not where.

JOHN DRYDEN (*Aurengzebe*, IV, 1)

368   Death

Death, be not proud, though some have callèd thee
Mighty and dreadful, for thou art not so;
For those whom thou think'st thou dost overthrow
Die not, poor Death; nor yet canst thou kill me.

189

From rest and sleep, which but thy pictures be,
Much pleasure; then from thee much more must flow;
And soonest our best men with thee do go—
Rest of their bones, and souls' delivery!
Thou art slave to fate, chance, kings, and desperate men,
And dost with poison, war, and sickness dwell;
And poppy or charms can make us sleep as well
And better than thy stroke. Why swell'st thou then?
One short sleep past, we wake eternally,
And Death shall be no more: Death, thou shalt die!

JOHN DONNE

369 *Verses Written in His Bible*

Even such is Time, that takes in trust
Our youth, our joys, our all we have,
And pays us but with earth and dust;
Who in the dark and silent grave
When we have wandered all our ways,
Shuts up the story of our days;
But from this earth, this grave, this dust,
My God shall raise me up, I trust.

SIR WALTER RALEIGH

370 *Heredity*

I am the family face;
Flesh perishes, I live on,
Projecting trait and trace
Through time to times anon,
And leaping from place to place
Over oblivion.

The years-heired feature that can
In curve and voice and eye
Despise the human span
Of durance—that is I;
The eternal thing in man,
That heeds no call to die.

THOMAS HARDY

7

MAN AND SOCIETY

Beginning with personal friendship, this section proceeds from the simpler to more complex forms of society. As contrasted with country and village life, the poetry brings before us the flux of courts, cities, and nations; the 'brittle glory' of kings and statesmen in different ages and continents; and such vigorous social life as that of seventeenth- and eighteenth-century London, when sharp character-studies were drawn in witty and vigorous verse. In poems towards the close of the section, the condition of the poorer classes of the community is felt as a tragedy and a challenge, to be met by reform or revolution. The section ends with contrasting hopes and fears concerning the basis, and the future, of all society, and of the civilizations devised by man.

---

371   *Parting at Morning*

Round the cape of a sudden came the sea,
And the sun looked over the mountain's rim:
And straight was a path of gold for him,
And the need of a world of men for me.

ROBERT BROWNING

372

When to the sessions of sweet silent thought
I summon up remembrance of things past,
I sigh the lack of many a thing I sought,
And with old woes new wail my dear time's waste:
Then can I drown an eye, unused to flow,
For precious friends hid in death's dateless night,
And weep afresh love's long since cancelled woe,

And moan the expense of many a vanished sight:
Then can I grieve at grievances foregone,
And heavily from woe to woe tell o'er
The sad account of fore-bemoanèd moan,
Which I new pay as if not paid before.
  But if the while I think on thee, dear friend,
  All losses are restored and sorrows end.

WILLIAM SHAKESPEARE

373   *Epigram*

To John I owed great obligation;
  But John unhappily thought fit
To publish it to all the nation;
  Sure John and I are more than quit.

MATTHEW PRIOR

374

Alas! they had been friends in youth;
But whispering tongues can poison truth;
And constancy lives in realms above;
And life is thorny; and youth is vain;
And to be wroth with one we love
Doth work like madness in the brain.
And thus it chanced, as I divine,
With Roland and Sir Leoline.
Each spake words of high disdain
And insult to his heart's best brother:
They parted—ne'er to meet again!
But never either found another
To free the hollow heart from paining:
They stood aloof, the scars remaining,
Like cliffs which had been rent asunder;
A dreary sea now flows between,
But neither heat, nor frost, nor thunder
Shall wholly do away, I ween,
The marks of that which once hath been.

SAMUEL TAYLOR COLERIDGE
(Christabel)

I have had playmates, I have had companions
In my days of childhood, in my joyful school-days;
All, all are gone, the old familiar faces.

I have been laughing, I have been carousing,
Drinking late, sitting late, with my bosom cronies;
All, all are gone, the old familiar faces.

I loved a Love once, fairest among women:
Closed are her doors on me, I must not see her—
All, all are gone, the old familiar faces.

I have a friend, a kinder friend has no man:
Like an ingrate, I left my friend abruptly;
Left him, to muse on the old familiar faces.

Ghost-like I paced round the haunts of my childhood,
Earth seem'd a desert I was bound to traverse,
Seeking to find the old familiar faces.

Friend of my bosom, thou more than a brother,
Why wert not thou born in my father's dwelling?
So might we talk of the old familiar faces.

How some they have died, and some they have left me,
And some are taken from me; all are departed;
All, all are gone, the old familiar faces.

                                        CHARLES LAMB

376   Written in Northampton County Asylum

I am! yet what I am who cares, or knows
    My friends forsake me like a memory lost.
I am the self-consumer of my woes;
    They rise and vanish, an oblivious host,
Shadows of life, whose very soul is lost.
And yet I am—I live—though I am tossed

Into the nothingness of scorn and noise,
    Into the living sea of waking dream,
Where there is neither sense of life, nor joys,
    But the huge shipwreck of my own esteem
And all that's dear. Even those I loved the best
Are strange—nay, they are stranger than the rest.

I long for scenes where man has never trod—
    For scenes where woman never smiled or wept—
There to abide with my Creator, God,
    And sleep as I in childhood sweetly slept,
Full of high thoughts, unborn. So let me lie,—
The grass below; above, the vaulted sky.

                                        JOHN CLARE

377

Were I a king, I might command content;
    Were I obscure, unknown should be my cares;
And were I dead, no thoughts should me torment,
    Nor words, nor wrongs, nor loves, nor hopes, nor fears.
A doubtful choice, of three things one to crave:
A kingdom, or a cottage, or a grave.

            EDWARD DE VERE, EARL OF OXFORD

378   From *The Village*

No; cast by Fortune on a frowning coast,
Which neither groves nor happy valleys boast;
Where other cares than those the Muse relates,
And other shepherds dwell with other mates:
By such examples taught, I paint the cot,
As Truth will paint it, and as bards will not.
Nor you, ye poor, of letter'd scorn complain,
To you the smoothest song is smooth in vain.
O'ercome by labour, and bow'd down by time,
Feel you the barren flattery of a rhyme?
Can poets soothe you, when you pine for bread,
By winding myrtles round your ruin'd shed?

Can their light tales your weighty griefs o'erpower,
  Or glad with airy mirth the toilsome hour?
    Lo! where the heath, with withering brake grown o'er
Lends the light turf that warms the neighbouring poor;
From thence a length of burning sand appears,
Where the thin harvest waves its wither'd ears;
Rank weeds, that every art and care defy,
Reign o'er the land, and rob the blighted rye:
There thistles stretch their prickly arms afar,
And to the ragged infant threaten war;
There poppies nodding, mock the hope of toil;
There the blue bugloss paints the sterile soil;
Hardy and high, above the slender sheaf,
The slimy mallow waves her silky leaf;
O'er the young shoot the charlock throws a shade,
And clasping tares cling round the sickly blade;
With mingled tints the rocky coasts abound,
And a sad splendour vainly shines around.

                              GEORGE CRABBE

379 From *Elegy Written in a Country Churchyard*

For them no more the blazing hearth shall burn,
  Or busy housewife ply her evening care:
No children run to lisp their sire's return,
  Or climb his knees the envied kiss to share.

Oft did the harvest to their sickle yield,
  Their furrow oft the stubborn glebe has broke:
How jocund did they drive their team afield!
  How bow'd the woods beneath their sturdy stroke! . . .

Perhaps in this neglected spot is laid
  Some heart once pregnant with celestial fire;
Hands, that the rod of empire might have sway'd
  Or waked to ecstasy the living lyre. . . .

Full many a gem of purest ray serene
  The dark unfathom'd caves of ocean bear:
Full many a flower is born to blush unseen,
  And waste its sweetness on the desert air.

Some village Hampden that with dauntless breast
    The little tyrant of his fields withstood,
Some mute inglorious Milton here may rest,
    Some Cromwell guiltless of his country's blood.

Th' applause of list'ning senates to command,
    The threats of pain and ruin to despise,
To scatter plenty o'er a smiling land,
    And read their history in a nation's eyes,

Their lot forbade: nor circumscrib'd alone
    Their growing virtues, but their crimes confin'd;
Forbade to wade through slaughter to a throne,
    And shut the gates of mercy on mankind. . . .

The thoughtless world to majesty may bow,
    Exalt the brave, and idolize success;
But more to innocence their safety owe
    Than power and genius e'er conspired to bless. . . .

THOMAS GRAY

380

'Is my team ploughing,
    That I was used to drive
And hear the harness jingle
    When I was man alive?'

Ay, the horses trample,
    The harness jingles now;
No change though you lie under
    The land you used to plough.

'Is football playing
    Along the river shore,
With lads to chase the leather,
    Now I stand up no more?'

Ay, the ball is flying,
    The lads play heart and soul,
The goal stands up, the keeper
    Stands up to keep the goal.

'Is my girl happy,
    That I thought hard to leave,
And has she tired of weeping
    As she lies down at eve?'

Ay, she lies down lightly,
    She lies not down to weep:
Your girl is well contented.
    Be still, my lad, and sleep.

'Is my friend hearty,
    Now I am thin and pine,
And has he found to sleep in
    A better bed than mine?'

Yes, lad, I lie easy,
    I lie as lads would choose;
I cheer a dead man's sweetheart,
    Never ask me whose.

ALFRED   EDWARD   HOUSMAN

381   *The Conformers*

Yes; we'll wed, my little fay,
    And you shall write you mine,
And in a villa chastely gray
    We'll house, and sleep, and dine.
    But those night-screened, divine,
    Stolen trysts of heretofore,
We of choice ecstasies and fine
            Shall know no more.

The formal faced cohue
    Will then no more upbraid
With smiting smiles and whisperings two
    Who have thrown less loves in shade.
    We shall no more evade
    The searching light of the sun,
Our game of passion will be played,
            Our dreaming done.

197

We shall go not in stealth
To rendezvous unknown,
But friends will ask me of your health,
And you about my own.
When we abide alone,
No leapings each to each,
But syllables in frigid tone
Of household speech.

When down to dust we glide
Men will not say askance,
As now: 'How all the country side
Rings with their mad romance!''
But as they graveward glance
Remark: 'In them we lose
A worthy pair, who helped advance
Sound parish views.'

THOMAS HARDY

382   *London in the Fifteenth Century*

Strong be thy wallis that about thee standis;
    Wise be the people that within thee dwellis;
Fresh is thy ryver with his lusty strandis;
    Blith be thy chirches, wele sownyng be thy bellis;
    Rich be thy merchauntis in substance that excellis;
Fair be their wives, right lovesom, white and small;
    Clere be thy virgyns, lusty under kellis:
London, thou art the flour of Cities all.

WILLIAM DUNBAR (*London*)

383   *Composed upon Westminster Bridge,
September 3, 1802*

Earth has not anything to show more fair:
Dull would he be of soul who could pass by
A sight so touching in its majesty:
This city now doth like a garment wear
The beauty of the morning; silent, bare,

Ships, towers, domes, theatres, and temples lie
Open unto the fields, and to the sky;
All bright and glittering in the smokeless air.
Never did sun more beautifully steep
In his first splendour valley, rock, or hill;
Ne'er saw I, never felt, a calm so deep!
The river glideth at his own sweet will:
Dear God! the very houses seem asleep;
And all that mighty heart is lying still!

WILLIAM WORDSWORTH

384   *London*

A mighty mass of brick, and smoke, and shipping,
   Dirty and dusky, but as wide as eye
Could reach, with here and there a sail just skipping
   In sight, then lost amidst the forestry
Of masts; a wilderness of steeples peeping
   On tiptoe through their sea-coal canopy;
A huge, dun cupola, like a foolscap crown
On a fool's head—and there is London Town!

LORD BYRON   (Don Juan, X)

385   *The Outskirts of London*

In the land of lobelias and tennis flannels
The rabbit shall burrow and the thorn revisit,
The nettle shall flourish on the gravel court,
And the wind shall say: 'Here were decent godless
   people:
Their only monument the asphalt road
And a thousand lost golf-balls.'

THOMAS STEARNS ELIOT   (The Rock)

386   *Athens and Palestine*

Satan to Christ

Behold

Where on the Aegean shore a city stands
Built nobly, pure the air, and light the soil,
Athens the eye of Greece, mother of arts

And eloquence, native to famous wits
Or hospitable, in her sweet recess,
City or suburban, studious walks and shades.
See there the olive-groves of Academe,
Plato's retirement, where the Attic bird
Trills her thick-warbled notes the summer long;
There flowery hill Hymettus with the sound
Of bees' industrious murmur oft invites
To studious musing; there Ilissus rolls
His whispering stream. Within the walls then view
The schools of ancient sages . . .
Thence to the famous orators repair,
Those ancient, whose resistless eloquence
Wielded at will that fierce democracy,
Shook the Arsenal and fulmined over Greece,
To Macedon, and Artaxerxes' throne. . . .
These here revolve, or, as thou lik'st, at home,
Till time mature thee to a kingdom's weight;
These rules will render thee a King complete
Within thyself, much more with empire joined.

Christ to Satan

Their orators thou then extoll'st, as those
The top of eloquence—statists indeed,
And lovers of their country, as may seem;
But herein to our prophets far beneath,
As men divinely taught, and better teaching
The solid rules of civil government
In their majestic, unaffected style
Than all the oratory of Greece and Rome.
In them is plainest taught, and easiest learnt,
What makes a nation happy, and keeps it so,
What ruins kingdoms, and lays cities flat;
These only, with our Law, best form a King.

JOHN MILTON

(*Paradise Regained*, IV)

How small, of all that human hearts endure,
That part which laws or kings can cause or cure!

SAMUEL JOHNSON
(lines added to GOLDSMITH's *Traveller*)

388　*Lucy Ashton's Song*

Look not thou on beauty's charming;
Sit thou still when kings are arming;
Taste not when the wine-cup glistens;
Speak not when the people listens;
Stop thine ear against the singer;
From the red gold keep thy finger;
Vacant heart and hand and eye,
Easy live and quiet die.

SIR WALTER SCOTT

389

I to my perils
　Of cheat and charmer
　Came clad in armour
　　By stars benign;
Hope lies to mortals
　And most believe her,
　But man's deceiver
　　Was never mine.

The thoughts of others
　Were light and fleeting,
　Of lovers' meeting
　　Or luck or fame;
Mine were of trouble
　And mine were steady,
　So I was ready
　　When trouble came.

ALFRED EDWARD HOUSMAN

I have lived
Riotously ill, like some that live in court,
And sometimes when my face was full of smiles
Have felt the maze of conscience in my breast.
Oft gay and honoured robes their tortures try:
We think caged birds sing when indeed they cry.

JOHN WEBSTER
(*The White Devil*, V, 4)

391

'Tis not a black coat and a little band,
A velvet-caped coat, faced before with serge,
And smelling to a nosegay all the day,
Or holding of a napkin in your hand,
Or saying a long grace at a table's end,
Or making low legs to a nobleman,
Or looking downward with your eyelids close,
And saying, 'Truly, an't may please your honour,'
Can get you any favour with great men;
You must be proud, bold, pleasant, resolute,
And now and then stab, as occasion serves.

CHRISTOPHER MARLOWE
(*Edward the Second*, II, 1)

392

The smiler with the knife under the cloak.

GEOFFREY CHAUCER
(*The Knight's Tale*)

393

So pitiful a thing is suitors' state!
Most miserable man, whom wicked fate
Hath brought to Court, to sue for had I wist
That few have found, and many one has missed!
Full little knowest thou, that hast not tried,

What hell it is in suing long to bide:
To lose good days, that might be better spent;
To waste long nights in pensive discontent;
To speed to-day, to be put back to-morrow;
To feed on hope, to pine with fear and sorrow;
To have thy Prince's grace, yet want her peers';
To have thy asking, yet wait many years;
To fret thy soul with crosses and with cares;
To eat thy heart through comfortless despairs;
To fawn, to crouch, to wait, to ride, to run,
To spend, to give, to want, to be undone.

EDMUND SPENSER

(*Mother Hubberd's Tale*)

394 *The Lot of the Poor Scholar*

Toil, envy, want, the Patron, and the jail.

SAMUEL JOHNSON

(*The Vanity of Human Wishes*)

395

For who would bear the whips and scorns of time,
The oppressor's wrong, the proud man's contumely,
The pangs of despised love, the law's delay,
The insolence of office, and the spurns
That patient merit of the unworthy takes,
When he himself might his quietus make
With a bare bodkin? who would fardels bear,
To grunt and sweat under a weary life,
But that the dread of something after death—
The undiscovered country, from whose bourn
No traveller returns,—puzzles the will,
And makes us rather bear those ills we have
Than fly to others that we know not of?

WILLIAM SHAKESPEARE (*Hamlet*, III, 1)

He says, *My reign is peace*, so slays
  A thousand in the dead of night.
Are you all happy now? he says,
  And those he leaves behind cry *quite*.
He swears he will have no contention,
  And sets all nations by the ears;
He shouts aloud, *No intervention!*
  Invades, and drowns them all in tears.

WALTER SAVAGE LANDOR

397   *Tamburlaine*

'And ride in triumph through Persepolis!'
Is it not brave to be a King, Techelles?
Usumcasane and Theridamas,
Is it not passing brave to be a King,
And ride in triumph through Persepolis?

CHRISTOPHER MARLOWE
(*Tamburlaine the Great*, First Part, I, 5)

398   *Caesar Receives from the King of Egypt*
the Head of Pompey

                   O thou conqueror,
Thou glory of the world once, now the pity,
Thou awe of nations, wherefore didst thou fall thus?
What poor fate follow'd thee and pluck'd thee on
To trust thy sacred life to an Egyptian?
The life and light of Rome to a blind stranger,
That honourable war ne'er taught a nobleness,
Nor worthy circumstance show'd what a man was;
That never heard thy name sung but in banquets
And loose lascivious pleasures; to a boy,
That hath no faith to comprehend thy greatness,
No study of thy life to know thy goodness:

And leave thy nation, nay, thy noble friend,
Leave him distrusted, that in tears falls with thee,
In soft relenting tears? Hear me, great Pompey,
If thy great spirit can hear, I must task thee:
Thou hast most unnobly robb'd me of my victory,
My love and mercy. . . .
Egyptians, dare you think your high pyramids,
Built to out-dure the sun as you suppose,
Where your unworthy kings lie rak'd in ashes,
Are monuments fit for him? No, brood of Nilus,
Nothing can cover his high fame but heaven,
No pyramids set off his memories
But the eternal substance of his greatness;
To which I leave him. Take the head away,
And with the body give it noble burial.

JOHN FLETCHER (*The False One*, II, 1)

399   *Ozymandias*

I met a traveller from an antique land
Who said: Two vast and trunkless legs of stone
Stand in the desert. Near them, on the sand,
Half sunk, a shattered visage lies, whose frown,
And wrinkled lip, and sneer of cold command,
Tell that its sculptor well those passions read
Which yet survive, stamped on these lifeless things,
The hand that mocked them and the heart that fed:
And on the pedestal these words appear:
'My name is Ozymandias, king of kings:
Look on my works, ye Mighty, and despair!'
Nothing beside remains. Round the decay
Of that colossal wreck, boundless and bare
The lone and level sands stretch far away.

PERCY BYSSHE SHELLEY

400   From *The Rubá'iyát of Omar Khayyám*

Think, in this batter'd Caravanserai
Whose Portals are alternate Night and Day,
    How Sultán after Sultán with his Pomp
Abode his destin'd Hour, and went his way.

They say the Lion and the Lizard keep
The Courts where Jamshýd gloried and drank deep:
   And Bahrám, that great Hunter—the Wild Ass
Stamps o'er his Head, but cannot break his Sleep.

I sometimes think that never blows so red
The Rose as where some buried Caesar bled;
   That every Hyacinth the Garden wears
Dropt in her Lap from some once lovely Head.

EDWARD FITZGERALD

401   *On the Tombs in Westminster Abbey*

Mortality, behold and fear!
What a change of flesh is here!
Think how many royal bones
Sleep within this heap of stones:
Here they lie had realms and lands,
Who now want strength to stir their hands:
Where from their pulpits seal'd with dust
They preach, 'In greatness is no trust.'
Here's an acre sown indeed
With the richest, royall'st seed
That the earth did e'er suck in
Since the first man died for sin:
Here the bones of birth have cried—
'Though gods they were, as men they died.'
Here are sands, ignoble things,
Dropt from the ruin'd sides of kings;
Here's a world of pomp and state,
Buried in dust, once dead by fate.

FRANCIS BEAUMONT

402   *The Farewell*

It was a' for our rightfu' King
   We left fair Scotland's strand;
It was a' for our rightfu' King
   We e'er saw Irish land,
      My dear—
   We e'er saw Irish land.

Now a' is done that men can do,
　　And a' is done in vain;
My love and native land, farewell!
　　For I maun cross the main,
　　　　My dear—
　　For I maun cross the main.

He turned him right and round about
　　Upon the Irish shore;
And gave his bridle-reins a shake,
　　With Adieu for evermore,
　　　　My dear—
　　With Adieu for evermore!

The sodger frae the war returns,
　　The sailor frae the main;
But I hae parted frae my love,
　　Never to meet again,
　　　　My dear—
　　Never to meet again.

When day is gane, and night is come,
　　And a' folk bound to sleep,
I think on him that's far awa',
　　The lee-lang night, and weep,
　　　　My dear—
　　The lee-lang night, and weep.

ROBERT BURNS

403　　*The Earl of Shaftesbury*

Of these the false Achitophel was first,
A name to all succeeding ages curst.
For close designs and crooked counsels fit,
Sagacious, bold, and turbulent of wit,
Restless, unfixed in principles and place,
In power unpleased, impatient of disgrace;
A fiery soul, which working out its way,
Fretted the pygmy body to decay
And o'er-informed the tenement of clay.

A daring pilot in extremity,
Pleased with the danger when the waves went high,
He sought the storms; but, for a calm unfit,
Would steer too nigh the sands to boast his wit.
Great wits are sure to madness near allied,
And thin partitions do their bounds divide;
Else why should he, with wealth and honours blest,
Refuse his age the needful hours of rest?
Punish a body which he could not please,
Bankrupt of life, yet prodigal of ease?
And all to leave what with his toil he won
To that unfeathered two-legged thing, a son;
Got while his soul did huddled notions try,
And born a shapeless lump like anarchy.
In friendship false, implacable in hate,
Resolved to ruin or to rule the State.

JOHN DRYDEN
(*Absalom and Achitophel*)

404   *George Villiers, Duke of Buckingham*

His Life

In the first rank of these did Zimri stand,
A man so various that he seemed to be
Not one, but all mankind's epitome.
Stiff in opinions, always in the wrong,
Was everything by starts, and nothing long;
But, in the course of one revolving moon,
Was chemist, fiddler, statesman, and buffoon;
Then all for women, painting, rhyming, drinking,
Besides ten thousand freaks that died in thinking.
Blest madman, who could every hour employ
With something new to wish, or to enjoy!
Railing and praising were his usual themes,
And both, to show his judgment, in extremes;
So over violent or over civil
That every man with him was God or Devil.
In squandering wealth was his peculiar art:
Nothing went unrewarded but desert.

Beggared by fools, whom still he found too late,
He had his jest, and they had his estate.
He laughed himself from court; then sought relief
By forming parties, but could n'er be chief;
For, spite of him, the weight of business fell
On Absalom and wise Achitophel;
Thus wicked but in will, of means bereft,
He left not faction, but of that was left.

JOHN DRYDEN
(*Absalom and Achitophel*)

His Death

In the worst inn's worst room, with mat half-hung,
The floors of plaster, and the walls of dung,
On once a flock-bed, but repair'd with straw,
With tape-ty'd curtains, never meant to draw,
The George and Garter dangling from that bed
Where tawdry yellow strove with dirty red,
Great Villiers lies—alas! how chang'd from him,
That life of pleasure, and that soul of whim!
Gallant and gay, in Cliveden's proud alcove,
The bow'r of wanton Shrewsbury and love;
Or just as gay, at council, in a ring
Of mimic'd statesmen, and their merry king.
No wit to flatter left of all his store!
No fool to laugh at, which he valu'd more.
There, victor of his health, of fortune, friends,
And fame, this lord of useless thousands ends.

ALEXANDER POPE (*Moral Essays*)

405   *Joseph Addison*

Peace to all such! but were there One whose fires
True Genius kindles, and fair Fame inspires;
Blest with each talent and each art to please,
And born to write, converse, and live with ease:
Should such a man, too fond to rule alone,
Bear, like the Turk, no brother near the throne,

View him with scornful, yet with jealous eyes,
And hate for arts that caus'd himself to rise;
Damn with faint praise, assent with civil leer,
And without sneering, teach the rest to sneer;
Willing to wound, and yet afraid to strike,
Just hint a fault, and hesitate dislike:
Alike reserv'd to blame, or to commend,
A tim'rous foe, and a suspicious friend;
Dreading ev'n fools, by flatterers besieg'd,
And so obliging, that he ne'er oblig'd;
Like Cato, give his little Senate laws,
And sit attentive to his own applause;
While Wits and Templars ev'ry sentence raise,
And wonder with a foolish face of praise—
Who but must laugh, if such a man there be?
Who would not weep, if Atticus were he!

ALEXANDER POPE
(Prologue to the Satires)

406   *In Memory of Eva Gore-Booth and
Con Markiewicz*

The light of evening, Lissadell,
Great windows open to the south,—
Two girls in silk kimonos, both
Beautiful, one a gazelle.
But a raving autumn shears
Blossom from the summer's wreath;
The older is condemned to death,
Pardoned, drags out lonely years
Conspiring among the ignorant.
I know not what the younger dreams—
Some vague Utopia—and she seems,
When withered old and skeleton-gaunt,
An image of such politics.
Many a time I think to seek
One or the other out and speak
Of that old Georgian mansion, mix
Pictures of the mind, recall
That table and the talk of youth,

Two girls in silk kimonos, both
Beautiful, one a gazelle.
Dear shadows, now you know it all,
All the folly of a fight
With a common wrong or right.
The innocent and the beautiful
Have no enemy but time;
Arise and bid me strike a match
And strike another till time catch;
Should the conflagration climb,
Run till all the sages know.
We the great gazebo built,
They convicted us of guilt;
Bid me strike a match and blow.

WILLIAM BUTLER YEATS

407   From *London*

And here a female atheist talks you dead.

SAMUEL JOHNSON

408   *Chloe*

'Yet Chloe sure was formed without a spot.'—
Nature in her then erred not, but forgot.
'With ev'ry pleasing, ev'ry prudent part,
Say, what can Chloe want?'—She wants a heart.
She speaks, behaves, and acts, just as she ought,
But never, never, reach'd one gen'rous thought.
Virtue she finds too painful an endeavour,
Content to dwell in decencies for ever.
So very reasonable, so unmov'd,
As never yet to love, or to be lov'd.
She, while her lover pants upon her breast,
Can mark the figures on an Indian chest;
And when she sees her friend in deep despair,
Observes how much a chintz exceeds mohair!
Forbid it, Heav'n, a favour or a debt
She e'er should cancel—but she may forget.
Safe is your secret still in Chloe's ear;

But none of Chloe's shall you ever hear.
Of all her dears she never slander'd one,
But cares not if a thousand are undone.
Would Chloe know if you're alive or dead?
She bids her footman put it in her head.
Chloe is prudent—would you too be wise?
Then never break your heart when Chloe dies.

ALEXANDER POPE (*Moral Essays*)

409

This one request I make to him that sits the clouds above:
That I were freely out of debt, as I am out of love.
Then for to dance, to drink, and sing, I should be very
willing;
I should not owe one lass a kiss, nor ne'er a knave a shilling.

'Tis only being in love and debt, that breaks us of our rest;
And he that is quite out of both, of all the world is blessed.
He sees the golden age, wherein all things were free and
common;
He eats, he drinks, he takes his rest, he fears no man nor
woman.

SIR JOHN SUCKLING

410 *The Latest Decalogue*

Thou shalt have one God only; who
Would be at the expense of two?
No graven images may be
Worshipped, except the currency:
Swear not at all; for, for thy curse
Thine enemy is none the worse:
At church on Sunday to attend
Will serve to keep the world thy friend:
Honour thy parents; that is, all
From whom advancement may befall:

Thou shalt not kill; but needst not strive
Officiously to keep alive:
Do not adultery commit;
Advantage rarely comes of it:
Thou shalt not steal; an empty feat,
When it's so lucrative to cheat:
Bear not false witness; let the lie
Have time on its own wings to fly:
Thou shalt not covet; but tradition
Approves all forms of competition.

ARTHUR HUGH CLOUGH

411

It is not to be thought of that the flood
   Of British freedom, which, to the open sea
   Of the world's praise, from dark antiquity
Hath flow'd, 'with pomp of waters, unwithstood,'—
Roused though it be full often to a mood
   Which spurns the check of salutary bands,—
   That this most famous stream in bogs and sands
Should perish; and to evil and to good
Be lost for ever. In our halls is hung
   Armoury of the invincible Knights of old:
We must be free or die, who speak the tongue
   That Shakespeare spake; the faith and morals hold
Which Milton held.—In everything we are sprung
   Of Earth's first blood, have titles manifold.

WILLIAM WORDSWORTH

412 Epitaph on Executed Patriots

Gladly we should rest ever, had we won
Freedom; we have lost, and very gladly rest.

ALGERNON CHARLES SWINBURNE,

from the Latin of WALTER SAVAGE LANDOR

Poor naked wretches, whereso'er you are,
That bide the pelting of this pitiless storm,
How shall your houseless heads and unfed sides,
Your loop'd and window'd raggedness, defend you
From seasons such as these? O, I have ta'en
Too little care of this! Take physic, pomp;
Expose thyself to feel what wretches feel,
That thou mayst shake the superflux to them,
And shew the heavens more just.

WILLIAM SHAKESPEARE
(*King Lear*, III, 4)

414   From *The Deserted Village*

Ill fares the land, to hastening ills a prey,
Where wealth accumulates, and men decay:
Princes and lords may flourish, or may fade;
A breath can make them, as a breath has made;
But a bold peasantry, their country's pride,
When once destroy'd, can never be supplied.
A time there was, ere England's griefs began,
When every rood of ground maintain'd its man;
For him light labour spread her wholesome store,
Just gave what life requir'd, but gave no more:
His blest companions, innocence and health;
And his best riches, ignorance of wealth. . . .
Ye friends to truth, ye statesmen who survey
The rich man's joy increase, the poor's decay,
'Tis yours to judge, how wide the limits stand
Between a splendid and a happy land.

OLIVER GOLDSMITH

415   *Two Merchants of Florence*

With her two brothers this fair lady dwelt,
　Enrichèd from ancestral merchandise,
And for them many a weary hand did swelt
　In torchèd mines and noisy factories,

214

And many once proud-quiver'd loins did melt
   In blood from stinging whip; with hollow eyes
Many all day in dazzling river stood,
To take the rich-ored driftings of the flood.

For them the Ceylon diver held his breath,
   And went all naked to the hungry shark;
For them his ears gush'd blood; for them in death
   The seal on the cold ice with piteous bark
Lay full of darts; for them alone did seethe
   A thousand men in troubles wide and dark:
Half-ignorant, they turn'd an easy wheel,
That set sharp racks at work, to pinch and peel.

JOHN KEATS (Isabella)

416   *In the Country near London*

Hark, the wind in the elm-boughs! from London it
   bloweth,
And telleth of gold, and of hope and unrest;
Of power that helps not; of wisdom that knoweth,
But teacheth not aught of the worst and the best. . . .

Hark, the March wind again of a people is telling;
Of the life that they live there, so haggard and grim,
That if we and our love amidst them had been dwelling,
My fondness had faltered, thy beauty grown dim.

This land we have loved in our love and our leisure
For them hangs in heaven, high out of their reach;
The wide hills o'er the sea-plain for them have no pleasure,
The grey homes of their fathers no story to teach.

The singers have sung and the builders have builded,
The painters have fashioned their tales of delight;
For what and for whom hath the world's book been gilded,
When all is for these but the blackness of night?

WILLIAM MORRIS
(The Message of the March Wind)

After they have tired of the brilliance of cities
And of striving for office where at last they may languish
Hung round with easy chains until
Death and Jerusalem glorify also the crossing-sweeper:
Then those streets the rich built and their easy love
Fade like old cloths, and it is death stalks through life
Grinning white through all faces
Clean and equal like the shine from snow.

In this time when grief pours freezing over us,
When the hard light of pain gleams at every street corner,
When those who were pillars of that day's gold roof
Shrink in their clothes; surely from hunger
We may strike fire, like fire from flint?
And our strength is now the strength of our bones
Clean and equal like the shine from snow
And the strength of famine and of our enforced idleness,
And it is the strength of our love for each other.

Readers of this strange language,
We have come at last to a country
Where light equal, like the shine from snow, strikes all faces,
Here you may wonder
How it was that works, money, interest, building, could
    ever hide
The palpable and obvious love of man for man.

Oh comrades, let not those who follow after
—The beautiful generation that shall spring from our
    sides—
Let not them wonder how after the failure of banks
The failure of cathedrals and the declared insanity of our
    rulers,
We lacked the Spring-like resources of the tiger
Or of plants who strike out new roots to gushing waters.
But through torn-down portions of old fabric let their eyes
Watch the admiring dawn explode like a shell
Around us, dazing us with light like snow.

STEPHEN SPENDER

For the labourer thou art bread
And a comely table spread,
From his daily labour come,
In a neat and happy home.

Thou art clothes, and fire, and food
For the trampled multitude!
No—in countries that are free
Such starvation cannot be,
As in England now we see. . . .

Thou art Justice—ne'er for gold
May thy righteous laws be sold,
As laws are in England:—thou
Shieldest alike the high and low. . . .

Thou art Love—the rich have kissed
Thy feet; and like him following Christ
Given their substance to the free,
And through the rough world follow thee . . .

Science, Poetry, and Thought,
Are thy Lamps; they make the lot
Of the dwellers in a cot
So serene, they curse it not. . . .

Men of England, Heirs of glory,
Heroes of unwritten story,
Nurslings of one mighty mother,
Hopes of her, and one another!

Rise, like lions after slumber,
In unvanquishable number,
Shake your chains to earth like dew,
Which in sleep had fallen on you!
Ye are many—they are few.

PERCY BYSSHE SHELLEY

(*The Masque of Anarchy*)

In vain, in vain—the all-composing hour
Resistless falls: the Muse obeys the Pow'r.
She comes! she comes! the sable throne behold
Of Night primaeval and of Chaos old!
Before her, Fancy's gilded clouds decay,
And all its varying rainbows die away.
Wit shoots in vain its momentary fires,
The meteor drops, and in a flash expires.
As one by one, at dread Medea's strain,
The sickening stars fade off th'ethereal plain;
As Argus' eyes, by Hermes' wand opprest,
Clos'd one by one to everlasting rest;
Thus at her felt approach, and secret might,
Art after Art goes out, and all is Night.
See skulking Truth to her old cavern fled,
Mountains of Casuistry heap'd o'er her head!
Philosophy, that lean'd on Heav'n before,
Shrinks to her second cause, and is no more.
Physic of Metaphysic begs defence,
And Metaphysic calls for aid on Sense!
See Mystery to Mathematics fly!
In vain! they gaze, turn giddy, rave, and die.
Religion blushing veils her sacred fires,
And unaware Morality expires.
Nor public flame, nor private, dares to shine;
Nor human spark is left, nor glimpse divine!
Lo! thy dread empire, Chaos, is restor'd;
Light dies before thy uncreating word;
Thy hand, great Anarch! lets the curtain fall,
And universal darkness buries all.

ALEXANDER POPE (*The Dunciad*)

420   *Meru*

Civilization is hooped together, brought
Under a rule, under the semblance of peace
By manifold illusion; but man's life is thought,
And he, despite his terror, cannot cease

Ravening through century after century,
Ravening, raging, and uprooting that he may come
Into the desolation of reality:
Egypt and Greece good-bye, and good-bye, Rome!
Hermits upon Mount Meru or Everest,
Caverned in night under the drifted snow,
Or where that snow and winter's dreadful blast
Beat down upon their naked bodies, know
That day brings round the night, that before dawn
His glory and his monuments are gone.

WILLIAM BUTLER YEATS

421

Which is the basest creature, Man or beast?
Birds feed on birds, beasts on each other prey,
But savage Man alone does Man betray.
Pressed by necessity, *they* kill for food:
Man undoes man, to do himself no good. . . .
For fear he arms, and is of arms afraid,
From fear to fear successively betrayed.

JOHN WILMOT, EARL OF ROCHESTER
(A Satire Against Mankind)

422

But vain the sword and vain the bow,
They never can work War's overthrow.
The hermit's prayer and the widow's tear
Alone can free the world from fear.

For a tear is an intellectual thing,
And a sigh is the sword of an Angel King,
And the bitter groan of the martyr's woe
Is an arrow from the Almighty's bow.

WILLIAM BLAKE   (The Grey Monk)

423 From *The Fall of Hyperion*

'None can usurp this height,' return'd that shade,
'But those to whom the miseries of the world
Are misery, and will not let them rest. . . .'
   'Are there not thousands in the world,' said I,
Encourag'd by the sooth voice of the shade,
'Who love their fellows even to the death,
Who feel the giant agony of the world,
And more, like slaves to poor humanity,
Labour for mortal good?'

JOHN KEATS

424 *Servants of Man*

—And ye shall die before your thrones be won.
—Yea, and the changed world and the liberal sun
  Shall move and shine without us, and we lie
    Dead; but if she too move on earth and live,
But if the old world with all the old irons rent
Laugh and give thanks, shall we be not content?
  Nay, we shall rather live, we shall not die,
    Life being so little and death so good to give. . . .

—Is this worth life, is this, to win for wages?
Lo, the dead mouths of the awful grey-grown ages,
  The venerable, in the past that is their prison,
    In the outer darkness, in the unopening grave,
Laugh, knowing how many as ye now say have said,
How many, and all are fallen, are fallen and dead:
  Shall ye dead rise, and these dead have not risen?
  —Not we but she, who is tender and swift to save.

—Are ye not weary and faint not by the way,
Seeing night by night devoured of day by day,
  Seeing hour by hour consumed in sleepless fire?
    Sleepless: and ye too, when shall ye too sleep?
—We are weary in heart and head, in hands and feet,
And surely more than all things sleep were sweet,
  Than all things save the inexorable desire
    Which whoso knoweth shall neither faint nor
    weep. . . .

—Pass on then and pass by us and let us be,
For what light think ye after life to see?
    And if the world fare better will ye know?
       And if man triumph who shall seek you and say?
—Enough of light is this for one life's span,
That all men born are mortal, but not man:
    And we men bring death lives by night to sow,
       That man may reap and eat and live by day.

ALGERNON CHARLES SWINBURNE

(*The Pilgrims*)

8

MAN AND GOD

In this final section we see, first, something of the evil, and of the good, which man has discerned in himself. From such facts men have arrived at conflicting findings about the nature of their world and the way in which they ought to live. In particular, their experience and opinions concerning a relationship between man and a power or powers outside himself have embraced doubt, indifference, or hostility on man's part; denial of any deity; and in contrast the Christian solution, which comprises poetry about the life and death of Jesus, fellowship with the risen Christ, and service in His Church. Beyond death, man has suspected a Divine Judgement, Hell, Purgatory, and Heaven, and he has written of these things with dread or joy. The section ends with poetry of prayer, of 'the dark night of the soul', and a mysticism which is not always imbued with Christian doctrines.

425

'There is no God,' the wicked saith,
   'And truly it's a blessing,
For what he might have done with us
   It's better only guessing.' . . .

Some others, also, to themselves
   Who scarce so much as doubt it,
Think there is none, when they are well,
   And do not think about it.

But country folks who live beneath
   The shadow of the steeple;
The parson and the parson's wife,
   And mostly married people;

Youths green and happy in first love,
   So thankful for illusion;
And men caught out in what the world
   Calls guilt, in first confusion;

And almost everyone when age,
   Disease, or sorrows strike him,
Inclines to think there is a God,
   Or something very like Him.

ARTHUR HUGH CLOUGH (Dipsychus)

426

An honest man's the noblest work of God.

ALEXANDER POPE (Essay on Man)

427

An honest God's the noblest work of man.

SAMUEL BUTLER (Notebooks)

428

As flies to wanton boys are we to the gods,
They kill us for their sport.

WILLIAM SHAKESPEARE
(King Lear, IV, 1)

429

The gods are just, and of our pleasant vices
Make instruments to plague us.

WILLIAM SHAKESPEARE
(King Lear, V, 3)

430

Now comes the pain of truth, to whom 'tis pain;
O folly! for to bear all naked truths,
And to envisage circumstance, all calm,
That is the top of sovereignty.

JOHN KEATS (Hyperion)

431

If way to the Better there be, it exacts a full look at the
worst.

THOMAS HARDY (In Tenebris)

In men, as in a rough-grown grove, remain
Cave-keeping evils that obscurely sleep.

WILLIAM SHAKESPEARE (*Lucrece*)

433

In me, past, present, future meet
To hold long chiding conference.
My lusts usurp the present tense
And strangle Reason in his seat.
My loves leap through the future's fence
To dance with dream-enfranchised feet.

In me the cave-man clasps the seer,
And garlanded Apollo goes
Chanting to Abraham's deaf ear.
In me the tiger sniffs the rose.
　　Look in my heart, kind friends, and tremble,
　　Since there your elements assemble.

SIEGFRIED SASSOON

434　　　*Timon Digs for Gold*

　　　　　　　Who dares, who dares,
In purity of manhood stand upright,
And say, 'This man's a flatterer'? if one be,
So are they all; for every grise of fortune
Is smooth'd by that below: the learnèd pate
Ducks to the golden fool: all is oblique;
There's nothing level in our cursèd natures
But direct villany . . .
This yellow slave
Will knit and break religions; bless the accurs'd;
Make the hoar leprosy ador'd; place thieves,
And give them title, knee and approbation,
With senators on the bench: this is it
That makes the wappen'd widow wed again;

She, whom the spital-house and ulcerous sores
Would cast the gorge at, this embalms and spices
To the April day again.

WILLIAM SHAKESPEARE
(*Timon of Athens*, IV, 3)

435 Ottima and Sebald in the Woods

Buried in woods we lay, you recollect;
Swift ran the searching tempest overhead;
And ever and anon some bright white shaft
Burned thro' the pine-tree roof, here burned and
    there,
As if God's messenger thro' the close wood screen
Plunged and replunged his weapon at a venture,
Feeling for guilty thee and me.

ROBERT BROWNING (*Pippa Passes*, I)

436   Satan in Hell

             What though the field be lost?
All is not lost; the unconquerable will,
And study of revenge, immortal hate,
And courage never to submit or yield,
And what is else not to be overcome. . . .
             Farewell, happy fields,
Where joy for ever dwells! Hail, horrors! hail
Infernal world! and thou profoundest Hell,
Receive thy new possessor—one who brings
A mind not to be changed by place or time:
The mind is its own place, and in itself
Can make a Heaven of Hell, a Hell of Heaven.
What matter where, if I be still the same,
And what I should be; all but less than he
Whom thunder hath made greater? Here at least
We shall be free: the Almighty hath not built
Here for his envy, will not drive us hence:
Here we may reign secure, and, in my choice,
To reign is worth ambition, though in Hell;
Better to reign in Hell, than serve in Heaven.

JOHN MILTON (*Paradise Lost*, I)

Whether we fall by ambition, blood, or lust,
Like diamonds we are cut with our own dust.

JOHN WEBSTER (*The Duchess of Malfi*, V, 5)

438　　　*Lost Days*

The lost days of my life until to-day
　　What were they, could I see them on the street
　　Lie as they fell? Would they be ears of wheat
Sown once for food but trodden into clay?
Or golden coins squandered and still to pay?
　　Or drops of blood dabbling the guilty feet?
　　Or such spilt water as in dreams must cheat
The undying throats of Hell, athirst alway?

I do not see them here; but after death
　　God knows I know the faces I shall see,
Each one a murdered self, with low last breath.
　　'I am thyself,—what hast thou done to me?'
'And I—and I—thyself', (lo! each one saith,)
　　'And thou thyself to all eternity!'

DANTE GABRIEL ROSSETTI

439　　　*A Hymn to God the Father*

Wilt Thou forgive that sin where I begun,
　　Which is my sin, though it were done before?
Wilt Thou forgive that sin, through which I run
　　And do run still, though still I do deplore?
　　　　When Thou hast done, Thou hast not done,
　　　　　For I have more.

Wilt Thou forgive that sin which I have won
　　Others to sin, and made my sin their door?
Wilt Thou forgive that sin which I did shun
　　A year or two, but wallowed in a score?
　　　　When Thou hast done, Thou hast not done,
　　　　　For I have more.

I have a sin of fear, that when I have spun
  My last thread, I shall perish on the shore;
But swear by Thyself that at my death Thy Son
  Shall shine as He shines now, and heretofore;
    And having done that, Thou hast done,
      I fear no more.

JOHN DONNE

440

Be vengeance wholly left to powers divine,
And let Heav'n judge betwixt your sons and mine:
If joys hereafter must be purchas'd here
With loss of all that mortals hold so dear,
Then welcome infamy and public shame,
And, last, a long farewell to worldly fame.
'Tis said with ease, but oh, how hardly tried
By haughty souls to human honour tied!
O, sharp convulsive pangs of agonizing pride!
Down then, thou rebel, never more to rise,
And what thou didst and dost so dearly prize,
That fame, that darling fame, make that thy sacrifice.
'Tis nothing thou hast given; then add thy tears
For a long race of unrepenting years:
'Tis nothing yet; yet all thou hast to give:
Then add those may-be years thou hast to live.
Yet nothing still: then poor and naked come,
Thy Father will receive his unthrift home,
And thy blest Saviour's blood discharge the mighty
  sum.

JOHN DRYDEN (*The Hind and the Panther*)

441

I wish to have no wishes left,
  But to leave all to Thee;
And yet I wish that Thou should'st will
  That which I wish should be.

FREDERICK WILLIAM FABER (*Hymn*)

227

Avenge, O Lord! thy slaughtered saints, whose bones
    Lie scattered on the Alpine mountains cold;
    Ev'n them who kept thy truth so pure of old
When all our fathers worship't stocks and stones,
Forget not: in thy book record their groans
    Who were thy sheep, and in their ancient fold
    Slain by the bloody Piedmontese, that rolled
Mother with infant down the rocks. Their moans
    The vales redoubled to the hills, and they
    To Heaven. Their martyred blood and ashes sow
O'er all th' Italian fields, where still doth sway
    The triple tyrant: that from these may grow
A hundred-fold, who, having learnt thy way,
    Early may fly the Babylonian woe.

JOHN MILTON

443   From *On the Russian Persecution of
the Jews*

Face loved of little children long ago,
    Head hated of the priests and rulers then,
Say, was not this thy Passion, to foreknow
    In death's worst hour the works of Christian men?

ALGERNON CHARLES SWINBURNE

444 Johannes Agricola in Meditation

There's heaven above, and night by night
    I look right through its gorgeous roof;
No suns and moons though e'er so bright
    Avail to stop me; splendour-proof
    I keep the broods of stars aloof:
For I intend to get to God,
    For 'tis to God I speed so fast,
For in God's breast, my own abode,
    Those shoals of dazzling glory, passed,
    I lay my spirit down at last.

I lie where I have always lain,
    God smiles as He has always smiled;
Ere suns and moons could wax and wane,
    Ere stars were thundergirt, or piled
    The heavens, God thought on me His child;
Ordained a life for me, arrayed
    Its circumstances every one
To the minutest; ay, God said
    This head this hand should rest upon
    Thus, ere He fashioned star or sun.
And having thus created me,
    Thus rooted me, He bade me grow,
Guiltless for ever, like a tree. . . .
I gaze below on hell's fierce bed,
    And those its waves of flame oppress,
    Swarming in ghastly wretchedness;
Whose life on earth aspired to be
    One altar-smoke, so pure!—to win
If not love like God's love to me,
    At least to keep His anger in;
    And all their striving turned to sin.
Priest, doctor, hermit, monk grown white
    With prayer, the broken-hearted nun,
The martyr, the wan acolyte,
    The incense-swinging child,—undone
    Before God fashioned star or sun!
God, whom I praise; how could I praise,
    If such as I might understand,
Make out and reckon on His ways,
    And bargain for His love, and stand,
    Paying a price, at His right hand?

ROBERT BROWNING

445   *Holy Willie's Prayer*

O Thou, that in the heavens dost dwell,
Wha, as it pleases best Thysel',
Sends ane to heaven an ten to hell,
        A' for Thy glory,
And no for onie guid or ill
        They've done afore Thee!

I bless and praise Thy matchless might,
When thousands Thou hast left in night,
That I am here afore Thy sight,
  For gifts an' grace
A burning and a shining light
  To a' this place.

What was I, or my generation,
That I should get sic exaltation,
I wha deserv'd most just damnation,
  For broken laws,
Sax thousand years ere my creation,
  Thro' Adam's cause.

When from my mither's womb I fell,
Thou might hae plung'd me deep in hell,
To gnash my gooms, and weep and wail,
  In burning lakes,
Where damnèd devils roar and yell,
  Chain'd to their stakes.

Yet I am here a chosen sample,
To show Thy grace is great and ample;
I'm here a pillar o' Thy temple,
  Strong as a rock,
A guide, a ruler, and example,
  To a' Thy flock.

But yet, O Lord! confess I must,
At times I'm fash'd wi' fleshly lust:
An' sometimes, too, in warldly trust
  Vile self gets in;
But Thou remembers we are dust,
  Defil'd wi' sin.

O Lord! yestreen, Thou kens, wi' Meg—
Thy pardon I sincerely beg;
O! may't ne'er be a livin plague
  To my dishonour,
An' I'll ne'er lift a lawless leg
  Again upon her. . . .

Maybe Thou lets this fleshly thorn
Buffet Thy servant e'en and morn,
Lest he owre proud and high shou'd turn,
    That he's sae gifted:
If sae, Thy han' maun e'en be borne,
    Until Thou lift it. . . .

ROBERT BURNS

446

Wine is good for shrivell'd lips,
    When a blanket wraps the day,
When the rotten woodland drips,
    And the leaf is stamp'd in clay. . . .

We are men of ruin'd blood;
    Therefore comes it we are wise.
Fish are we that love the mud,
    Rising to no fancy-flies. . . .

Virtue!—to be good and just—
    Every heart, when sifted well,
Is a clot of warmer dust,
    Mix'd with cunning sparks of hell. . . .

Fill the can, and fill the cup:
    All the windy ways of men
Are but dust that rises up,
    And is lightly laid again.

ALFRED, LORD TENNYSON
(The Vision of Sin)

447

But when we in our viciousness grow hard,—
O misery on't!—the wise gods seel our eyes;
In our own filth drop our clear judgments.

WILLIAM SHAKESPEARE
(Antony and Cleopatra, III, 11)

448

To each his sufferings: all are men,
    Condemn'd alike to groan;
The tender for another's pain,
    The unfeeling for his own.

THOMAS GRAY
(*Ode on a Distant Prospect of Eton College*)

449

That best portion of a good man's life,
His little, nameless, unremembered acts
Of kindness and of love.

WILLIAM WORDSWORTH (*Tintern Abbey*)

450

His virtues walk'd their narrow round,
    Nor made a pause, nor left a void;
And sure the Eternal Master found
    His single talent well employ'd.

SAMUEL JOHNSON
(*On the Death of Mr. Levett*)

451 *Duncan*

His virtues
Will plead like angels, trumpet-tongu'd, against
The deep damnation of his taking-off.

WILLIAM SHAKESPEARE
(*Macbeth*, I, 7)

452 *Demogorgon to Prometheus*

To suffer woes which Hope thinks infinite;
To forgive wrongs darker than death or night;
    To defy Power, which seems omnipotent;
To love, and bear; to hope till Hope creates

From its own wreck the thing it contemplates;
  Neither to change, nor falter, nor repent;
This, like thy glory, Titan, is to be
Good, great and joyous, beautiful and free;
This is alone Life, Joy, Empire, and Victory.

PERCY BYSSHE SHELLEY
(*Prometheus Unbound*, IV)

453　*The Old Stoic*

Riches I hold in light esteem,
  And Love I laugh to scorn;
And lust of fame was but a dream
  That vanished with the morn:

And, if I pray, the only prayer
  That moves my lips for me
Is, 'Leave the heart that now I bear,
  And give me liberty!'

Yes, as my swift days near their goal,
  'Tis all that I implore:
In life and death a chainless soul,
  With courage to endure.

EMILY JANE BRONTË

454

Give me a spirit that on life's rough sea
Loves t' have his sails filled with a lusty wind,
E'en till his sail-yards tremble, his masts crack,
And his rapt ship run on her side so low
That she drinks water and her keel ploughs air.
There is no danger to a man that knows
What life and death is; there's not any law
Exceeds his knowledge: neither is it lawful
That he should stoop to any other law.
He goes before them, and commands them all,
That to himself is a law rational.

GEORGE CHAPMAN
(*The Conspiracy of Byron*, III, 1)

Strange the world about me lies,
   Never yet familiar grown—
Still disturbs me with surprise,
   Haunts me like a face half-known.

In this house with starry dome,
   Floored with gemlike plains and seas,
Shall I never feel at home,
   Never wholly be at ease?

On from room to room I stray,
   Yet my Host can ne'er espy,
And I know not to this day
   Whether guest or captive I.

So, between the starry dome
   And the floor of plains and seas,
I have never felt at home,
   Never wholly been at ease.

SIR WILLIAM WATSON

456   *Destiny*

Why each is striving, from of old,
To love more deeply than he can?
Still would be true, yet still grows cold?
—Ask of the Powers that sport with man!

They yok'd in him, for endless strife,
A heart of ice, a soul of fire;
And hurl'd him on the Field of Life,
An aimless unallay'd Desire.

MATTHEW ARNOLD

457   *Hap*

If but some vengeful god would call to me
From up the sky, and laugh: 'Thou suffering thing,
Know that thy sorrow is my ecstasy,
That thy love's loss is my hate's profiting!'

Then would I bear, and clench myself, and die,
Steeled by the sense of ire unmerited; .
Half-eased in that a Powerfuller than I
Had willed and meted me the tears I shed.

But not so. How arrives it joy lies slain,
And why unblooms the best hope ever sown?
—Crass Casualty obstructs the sun and rain,
And dicing Time for gladness casts a moan. . . .
These purblind Doomsters had as readily strown
Blisses about my pilgrimage as pain.

THOMAS HARDY

458

Though in our miseries Fortune have a part,
Yet in our noble sufferings she hath none:
Contempt of pain, that we may call our own.

JOHN WEBSTER (*The Duchess of Malfi*, V, 3)

459 *Adam and Eve in Eden*

Heaven may prevent that ill He does foresee;
And, not preventing, though He does not cause,
He seems to will that men should break his laws. . . .
The laws were hard, the power to keep them weak.
Did we solicit Heaven to mould our clay?
From darkness to produce us to the day?
Did we concur to life, or choose to be?
Was it our will which formed, or was it He?
Since 'twas His choice, not ours, which placed us here,
The laws we did not choose why should we bear?

JOHN DRYDEN (*The State of Innocence*)

460 From *Rubá'iyát of Omar Khayyám*

But leave the Wise to wrangle, and with me
The Quarrel of the Universe let be:
    And, in some corner of the Hubbub coucht,
Make Game of that which makes as much of Thee. . . .

Oh Thou, who didst with pitfall and with gin
Beset the Road I was to wander in,
   Thou wilt not with Predestined Evil round
Enmesh, and then impute my Fall to Sin!

Oh Thou, who Man of baser Earth didst make,
And ev'n with Paradise devise the Snake:
   For all the Sin wherewith the Face of Man
Is blacken'd—Man's forgiveness give—and take!

EDWARD FITZGERALD

461

But if nor Christ nor Odin help, why then
Still at the worst are we the sons of men.

WILLIAM MORRIS
(The Earthly Paradise: The Lovers of Gudrun)

462

A creed is a rod,
   And a crown is of night;
But this thing is God,
   To be man with thy might,
To grow straight in the strength of thy spirit, and
     live out thy life as the light. . . .

Lo, winged with world's wonders,
   With miracles shod,
With the fires of his thunders
   For raiment and rod,
God trembles in heaven, and his angels are white
     with the terror of God.

For his twilight is come on him,
   His anguish is here;
And his spirits gaze dumb on him,
   Grown grey from his fear;
And his hour taketh hold on him stricken, the last
     of his infinite year.

Thought made him and breaks him,
　　Truth slays and forgives;
But to you, as time takes him,
　　This new thing it gives,
Even love, the beloved Republic, that feeds upon
　　freedom and lives.

ALGERNON CHARLES SWINBURNE (*Hertha*)

463

A power from the unknown God,
　　A Promethean conqueror, came;
Like a triumphal path he trod
　　The thorns of death and shame.
　　　A mortal shape to him
　　　Was like the vapour dim
Which the orient planet animates with light;
　　　Hell, Sin, and Slavery came,
　　　Like bloodhounds mild and tame,
Nor preyed until their Lord had taken flight.
　　　The moon of Mahomet
　　　Arose, and it shall set:
While, blazoned as on heaven's immortal noon,
　　The Cross leads generations on.

PERCY BYSSHE SHELLEY (*Hellas*)

464　　　*Saint John Baptist*

The last and greatest Herald of Heaven's King,
Girt with rough skins, hies to the deserts wild,
Among that savage brood the woods forth bring,
Which he than man more harmless found and mild.
His food was locusts, and what young doth spring
With honey that from virgin hives distill'd;
Parch'd body, hollow eyes, some uncouth thing
Made him appear, long since from earth exiled.
There burst he forth: 'All ye, whose hopes rely
On God, with me amidst these deserts mourn;

237

Repent, repent, and from old errors turn!'
—Who listen'd to his voice, obey'd his cry?
  Only the echoes, which he made relent,
  Rung from their marble caves 'Repent! Repent!'

WILLIAM DRUMMOND

465   *The Birth of Jesus*

He came al so still
  There his mother was,
As dew in April
  That falleth on the grass.

He came al so still
  To his mother's bower,
As dew in April
  That falleth on the flower.

He came al so still
  There his mother lay,
As dew in April
  That falleth on the spray.

ANONYMOUS (15th century) (Carol)

466   From *A Christmas Carol*

We see Him come, and know Him ours,
Who with His sunshine and His showers
Turns all the patient ground to flowers.

ROBERT HERRICK

467

The best of men
That e'er wore earth about him, was a sufferer,
A soft, meek, patient, humble, tranquil spirit;
The first true gentleman that ever breathed.

THOMAS DEKKER
(The Honest Whore, First Part, I, 2)

Those holy fields
Over whose acres walked those blessed feet
Which, fourteen hundred years ago, were nailed
For our advantage on the bitter cross.

WILLIAM SHAKESPEARE
(King Henry IV, First Part, I, 1)

469   ### Redemption

Having been tenant long to a rich Lord,
  Not thriving, I resolvèd to be bold,
  And make a suit unto him to afford
A new small-rented lease, and cancel the old.
In Heaven at His manor I Him sought;
  They told me there, that He was lately gone
  About some land, which He had dearly bought
Long since on Earth, to take possession.

I straight returned, and knowing His great birth,
  Sought Him accordingly in great resorts,
  In cities, theatres, gardens, parks and courts:
At length I heard a ragged noise and mirth
  Of thieves and murderers. There I Him espied,
  Who straight, 'Your suit is granted,' said, and died.

GEORGE HERBERT

470

Thy hands to give Thou can'st not lift,
  Yet will Thy hand still giving be;
It gives, but, oh, itself's the gift!
  It gives tho' bound, tho' bound 'tis free!

RICHARD CRASHAW
(Upon the Bleeding Crucifix)

Drop, drop, slow tears,
   And bathe those beauteous feet
Which brought from Heaven
   The news and Prince of Peace;
Cease not, wet eyes,
   His mercy to entreat;
To cry for vengeance
   Sin doth never cease.
In your deep floods
   Drown all my faults and fears:
Nor let His eye
   See sin, but through my tears.

PHINEAS FLETCHER

472

Thy grave! To which my thoughts shall move
   Like bees in storms unto their hive;
That from the murd'ring world's false love
   Thy death may keep my soul alive.

HENRY VAUGHAN (*The Obsequies*)

473   From *Easter*

I got me flowers to straw Thy way,
   I got me boughs off many a tree;
But Thou wast up by break of day,
   And brought'st Thy sweets along with Thee.

GEORGE HERBERT

474   From *Resurrection*

Sleep, sleep, old sun! thou canst not have repast,
As yet, the wound thou took'st on Friday last;
Sleep, then, and rest; the world may bear thy stay,
A better Sun rose before thee to-day,
Who, not content to enlighten all that dwell
On the earth's face, as thou, enlightened hell,
And made the dark fires languish in that vale.

JOHN DONNE

Suddenly
A sharp bell rang from close beside the door,
   And I leapt up when something pass'd me by,

Shrill ringing going with it; still half blind
   I staggered after; a great sense of awe
At every step kept gathering on my mind.
   Thereat I have no marvel, for I saw

One sitting on the altar as a throne
   Whose face no man could say he did not know;
And though the bell still rang, he sat alone,
   With raiment half blood-red, half white as snow. . . .

But mightily the gentle voice came down:
   'Rise up, and look and listen, Galahad,
Good knight of God, for you will see no frown
   Upon my face; I come to make you glad.

For that you say that you are all alone,
   I will be with you always, and fear not
You are uncared-for, though no maiden moan
   Above your empty tomb; for Launcelot,

He in good time shall be my servant too;
   Meantime, take note whose sword first made him
     knight,
And who has loved him alway, yea, and who
   Still trusts him alway, though in all men's sight

He is just what you know, O Galahad.
   This love is happy even as you say,
But would you for a little time be glad,
   To make ME sorry long, day after day?

Her warm arms round his neck half throttle ME,
   The hot love-tears burn deep like spots of lead,
Yea, and the years pass quick: right dismally
   Will Launcelot at one time hang his head;

Yea, old and shrivell'd he shall win my love.'
           WILLIAM MORRIS (*Sir Galahad*)

Look unto mine handës, man!
These gloves were given me when I her sought;
They be not white, but red and wan;
Embroidered with blood my spouse them
    bought. . . .

Long and love thou never so high,
Yet is my love more than thine may be.
Thou gladdest, thou weepest, I sit thee by:
Yet might thou, spouse, look once at me!

ANONYMOUS (15th century)
(Quia Amore Langueo)

477

Spit in my face, you Jews, and pierce my side,
Buffet, and scoff, scourge, and crucify me,
For I have sinn'd, and sinn'd, and only He,
Who could do no iniquity, hath died.
But by my death can not be satisfied
My sins, which pass the Jews' impiety.
They kill'd once an inglorious man, but I
Crucify him daily, being now glorified.
O let me then His strange love still admire;
Kings pardon, but He bore our punishment;
And Jacob came cloth'd in vile harsh attire,
But to supplant, and with gainful intent;
God cloth'd Himself in vile man's flesh, that so
He might be weak enough to suffer woe.

JOHN DONNE

478   *The Poor Parson*

A good man was there of religion,
And was a poorë Parson of a town;
But rich he was of holy thought and work . . .
Wide was his parish, and houses far asunder,
But he ne leftë not for rain ne thunder,

In sickness nor in mischief to visite
The farthest in his parish, much and lite,
Upon his feet, and in his hand a staff.
This noble example to his sheep he gave
That first he wrought and afterward he taught.
Out of the Gospel he those wordës caught,
And this figure he added eke thereto,
That if gold rustë what shall iron do? . . .
And though he holy were and virtuous,
He was to sinful man not despitous,
Nor of his speechë dangerous ne digne,
But in his teaching discreet and benign.
To drawen folk to Heaven by fairness,
By good example, this was his business:
But it were any person obstinate,
What so he were, of high or low estate,
Him would he snybben sharply for the nonce.
A better priest I trow that nowhere none is:
He waited after no pomp and reverence,
Ne maked him a spicëd conscience,
But Christës lore, and his Apostles twelve,
He taught, but first he followed it himself.

GEOFFREY CHAUCER
(*Prologue to the Canterbury Tales*)

479   *The Village Clergyman*

A man he was to all the country dear,
And passing rich with forty pounds a year;
Remote from towns he ran his godly race,
Nor e'er had changed, nor wished to change his place;
Unpractised he to fawn, or seek for power,
By doctrines fashioned to the varying hour;
Far other aims his heart had learned to prize,
More skilled to raise the wretched than to rise.
His house was known to all the vagrant train;
He chid their wanderings, but relieved their pain. . . .
Pleased with his guests, the good man learned to glow,
And quite forgot their vices in their woe;
Careless their merits or their faults to scan
His pity gave ere charity began.

Thus to relieve the wretched was his pride,
And e'en his failings leaned to Virtue's side;
But in his duty prompt at every call,
He watched and wept, he prayed and felt, for all;
And, as a bird each fond endearment tries
To tempt its new-fledged offspring to the skies,
He tried each art, reproved each dull delay,
Allured to brighter worlds, and led the way.

OLIVER GOLDSMITH
(*The Deserted Village*)

480 *Passing Away*

Passing away, saith the World, passing away:
Chances, beauty and youth sapped day by day:
Thy life never continueth in one stay.
Is the eye waxen dim, is the dark hair changing to gray
That hath won neither laurel nor bay?
I shall clothe myself in Spring and bud in May:
Thou, root-stricken, shalt not rebuild thy decay
On my bosom for aye.
Then I answered: Yea.

Passing away, saith my Soul, passing away:
With its burden of fear and hope, of labour and play,
Hearken what the past doth witness and say:
Rust in thy gold, a moth is in thine array,
A canker is in thy bud, thy leaf must decay.
At midnight, at cockcrow, at morning, one certain day,
Lo, the Bridegroom shall come and shall not delay:
Watch thou and pray.
Then I answered: Yea.

Passing away, saith my God, passing away:
Winter passeth after the long delay:
New grapes on the vine, new figs on the tender spray,
Turtle calleth turtle in Heaven's May.
Though I tarry, wait for me, trust me, watch and pray.
Arise, come away; night is past, and lo, it is day;
My love, my sister, my spouse, thou shalt hear me say—
Then I answered: Yea.

CHRISTINA GEORGINA ROSSETTI

Hatred and vengeance, my eternal portion,
Scarce can endure delay of execution,
Wait, with impatient readiness, to seize my
                  Soul in a moment.

Damn'd below Judas: more abhorr'd than he was,
Who for a few pence sold his holy Master.
Twice betrayed Jesus me, the last delinquent,
                  Deems the profanest.

Man disavows, and Deity disowns me:
Hell might afford my miseries a shelter;
Therefore Hell keeps her ever hungry mouths all
                  Bolted against me. . . .

WILLIAM COWPER

482   *Soliloquy of Faustus*

Ah, Faustus,
Now hast thou but one bare hour to live,
And then thou must be damn'd perpetually!
Stand still, you ever-moving spheres of heaven,
That time may cease, and midnight never come;
Fair Nature's eye, rise, rise again, and make
Perpetual day; or let this hour be but
A year, a month, a week, a natural day,
That Faustus may repent and save his soul!
O lente, lente currite, noctis equi!
The stars move still, time runs, the clock will strike,
The devil will come, and Faustus must be damn'd.
O, I'll leap up to my God!—Who pulls me down?—
See, see, where Christ's blood streams in the firmament!
One drop would save my soul, half a drop: ah, my Christ!—
Ah, rend not my heart for naming of my Christ!
Yet will I call on him: O spare me, Lucifer!—

Where is it now! 'tis gone: and see, where God
Stretcheth out his arm, and bends his ireful brows!
Mountains and hills, come, come, and fall on me,
And hide me from the heavy wrath of God! . . .

CHRISTOPHER MARLOWE

(*Doctor Faustus*, V, 2)

483 *Claudio under Sentence of Death*

Ay, but to die, and go we know not where;
To lie in cold obstruction, and to rot;
This sensible warm motion to become
A kneaded clod; and the delighted spirit
To bathe in fiery floods, or to reside
In thrilling region of thick-ribbèd ice;
To be imprison'd in the viewless winds,
And blown with restless violence round about
The pendent world; or to be worse than worst
Of those that lawless and incertain thoughts
Imagine howling!—'tis too horrible!
The weariest and most loathèd worldly life
That age, ache, penury, and imprisonment
Can lay on nature, is a paradise
To what we fear of death.

WILLIAM SHAKESPEARE

(*Measure for Measure*, III, 1)

484 From '*They Are All Gone . . .*'

They are all gone into the world of light!
   And I alone sit ling'ring here;
Their very memory is fair and bright,
      And my sad thoughts doth clear. . . .

I see them walking in an air of glory,
   Whose light doth trample on my days:
My days, which are at best but dull and hoary,
      Mere glimmering and decays. . . .

Dear, beauteous Death! the jewel of the just,
    Shining nowhere but in the dark;
What mysteries do lie beyond thy dust,
        Could man outlook that mark!

He that hath found some fledg'd bird's nest may know
    At first sight if the bird be flown;
But what fair well or grove he sings in now,
        That is to him unknown.

And yet, as angels in some brighter dreams
    Call to the soul when man doth sleep,
So some strange thoughts transcend our wonted themes,
        And into glory peep.
                                    HENRY VAUGHAN

485

I saw Eternity the other night,
Like a great ring of pure and endless light,
        All calm, as it was bright;
And round beneath it, Time in hours, days, years,
        Driven by the spheres
Like a vast shadow moved; in which the world
        And all her train were hurled.
                        HENRY VAUGHAN (*The World*)

486

The whole round world is not eno' to fill
The heart's three corners; but it craveth still.
Only the Trinity, that made it, can
Suffice the vast-triangled heart of man.
                CHRISTOPHER HARVEY (*Schola Cordis*)

487

Whoso has felt the Spirit of the Highest
    Cannot confound nor doubt Him nor deny;
Yea with one voice, O world, tho' thou deniest,
    Stand thou on that side, for on this am I.
FREDERIC WILLIAM HENRY MYERS (*St. Paul*)

Hear the voice of the Bard!
Who present, past, and future, sees;
   Whose ears have heard
   The Holy Word
That walk'd among the ancient trees,

Calling the lapsèd soul,
And weeping in the evening dew;
   That might control
   The starry pole,
And fallen, fallen light renew!

'O Earth, O Earth, return!
Arise from out the dewy grass;
   Night is worn,
   And the morn
Rises from the slumberous mass.

'Turn away no more:
Why wilt thou turn away?
   The starry floor,
   The wat'ry shore,
Is giv'n thee till the break of day.'

WILLIAM BLAKE

489

No worst, there is none. Pitched past pitch of grief,
More pangs will, schooled at forepangs, wilder wring.
Comforter, where, where is your comforting?
Mary, mother of us, where is your relief?
My cries heave, herds-long; huddle in a main, a chief
Woe, world-sorrow; on an age-old anvil wince and
      sing—
Then lull, then leave off. Fury had shrieked 'No ling-
ering! Let me be fell: force I must be brief.'

O the mind, mind has mountains; cliffs of fall
Frightful, sheer, no-man-fathomed. Hold them cheap
May who ne'er hung there. Nor does long our small
Durance deal with that steep or deep. Here! creep,
Wretch, under a comfort serves in a whirlwind: all
Life death does end and each day dies with sleep.

GERARD MANLEY HOPKINS

490   *To Saint Teresa*

O sweet incendiary! show here thy art,
Upon this carcase of a hard cold heart. . . .
O thou undaunted daughter of desires!
By all thy dower of lights and fires;
By all the eagle in thee, all the dove;
By all thy lives and deaths of love;
By thy large draughts of intellectual day,
And by thy thirsts of love more large than they;
By all thy brim-filled bowls of fierce desire,
By thy last morning's draught of liquid fire;
By the full kingdom of that final kiss
That seized thy parting soul, and sealed thee His;
By all the Heavens thou hast in Him—
Fair sister of the seraphim!—
By all of Him we have in thee;
Leave nothing of myself in me.
Let me so read thy life, that I
Unto all life of mine may die.

RICHARD CRASHAW

(The Flaming Heart)

491

The world, the clustering spheres, He made;
The glorious light, the soothing shade,
    Dale, champaign, grove, and hill;
The multitudinous abyss,
Where Secrecy remains in bliss,
    And Wisdom hides her skill. . . .

Strong is the horse upon his speed;
Strong in pursuit the rapid glede,
    Which makes at once his game:
Strong the tall ostrich on the ground;
Strong through the turbulent profound
    Shoots xiphias to his aim.

Strong is the lion—like a coal
His eyeball—like a bastion's mole
    His chest against the foes:
Strong, the gier-eagle on his sail,
Strong against tide, the enormous whale
    Emerges as he goes.

But stronger still in earth and air,
And in the sea the man of prayer,
    And far beneath the tide:
And in the seat to faith assigned,
Where ask is have, where seek is find,
    Where knock is open wide.

CHRISTOPHER SMART
(*Song to David*)

492   *Prayer*

Prayer, the Church's banquet, angels' age,
God's breath in man returning to his birth. . . .
The milky way, the bird of Paradise,
Church-bells beyond the stars heard, the soul's blood,
The land of spices; something understood.

GEORGE HERBERT (*Prayer*)

493

           And I have felt
A presence that disturbs me with the joy
Of elevated thoughts; a sense sublime
Of something far more deeply interfused,
Whose dwelling is the light of setting suns,
And the round ocean and the living air,
And the blue sky, and in the mind of man.

WILLIAM WORDSWORTH (*Tintern Abbey*)

Still let my tyrants know, I am not doom'd to wear
Year after year in gloom and desolate despair;
A messenger of Hope comes every night to me,
And offers, for short life, eternal liberty.

He comes with Western winds, with evening's wandering
    airs,
With that clear dusk of heaven that brings the thickest stars:
Winds take a pensive tone, and stars a tender fire,
And visions rise, and change, that kill me with desire.

Desire for nothing known in my maturer years,
When Joy grew mad with awe, at counting future tears:
When, if my spirit's sky was full of flashes warm,
I knew not whence they came, from sun or thunder-storm.

But first, a hush of peace—a soundless calm descends;
The struggle of distress and fierce impatience ends.
Mute music soothes my breast—unutter'd harmony
That I could never dream, till Earth was lost to me.

Then dawns the Invisible; the Unseen its truth reveals;
My outward sense is gone, my inward essence feels;
Its wings are almost free—its home, its harbour found,
Measuring the gulf, it stoops, and dares the final bound.

O dreadful is the check—intense the agony—
When the ear begins to hear, and the eye begins to see;
When the pulse begins to throb—the brain to think again—
The soul to feel the flesh, and the flesh to feel the chain.

Yet I would lose no sting, would wish no torture less;
The more that anguish racks, the earlier it will bless;
And robed in fires of hell, or bright with heavenly shine,
If it but herald Death, the vision is divine.

EMILY JANE BRONTË

Tho' thou art worshipped by the names divine
  Of Jesus and Jehovah, thou art still
The Son of Morn in weary Night's decline,
  The lost traveller's dream under the hill.

WILLIAM BLAKE

(The Gates of Paradise)

496 *The Moths Send Messengers to Their God*

Then went a Third, who spurr'd with true Desire,
Plunging at once into the sacred Fire,
Folded his Wings within, till he became
One Colour and one Substance with the Flame.
He only knew the Flame who in it burn'd;
And only He could tell who ne'er to tell return'd.

EDWARD FITZGERALD

(after ATTAR's Bird-Parliament)

NOTES

No. 4, p. 15. *crudded rack:* curdled (congealed) cloud. *Arion:* A Greek poet and musician who, when sailors threatened to murder him, according to legend threw himself overboard and was brought ashore by a dolphin which his music had attracted.

No. 6, p. 15. *Lucifer:* The morning star of the Greeks; the planet Venus when seen in the morning before dawn. In later times Lucifer was identified with Satan.

No. 7, p. 16. *Phaeton:* the son of Helios (the Sun). He induced his father to allow him to drive the chariot of the sun across heavens for one day. He could not, however, manage the horses, and, as he threatened to destroy the earth, Zeus consumed him with a flash of lightning.

No. 9, p. 17. *Jacob's dream:* see Book of Genesis, Chapter 28.

No. 11, p. 18. *yestreen:* yesterday evening; *laith:* loath; *lang owre:* long before; *aboon:* above; *kems:* combs; *haf owre:* half over.

No. 12, p. 19. *The Titanic:* On April 15, 1912, the White Star liner *Titanic*, at that time the largest vessel afloat, was on her maiden voyage across the Atlantic, when she sank after striking an iceberg. Of the 2,224 persons on board, 1,513 were lost.

No. 15, p. 23. The *Revenge:* the ship in which Sir Richard Grenville met his death in 1591 after his gallant fight with fifty-three Spanish ships.

No. 16, p. 24, 'The Battle of the Baltic': In 1801, while England and France were at war, Denmark, Sweden, and Russia combined in a policy of armed neutrality to resist the British claim to search neutral vessels for cargoes of French goods. An English fleet under Admiral Parker, with Nelson as second in command, was sent to attack the Danish fleet at Copenhagen.

No. 18, p. 25. *Ulysses:* The hero whose Greek name was Odysseus, and whose adventures after the fall of Troy form the subject of Homer's 'Odyssey,' is depicted in Tennyson's monologue in his old age after his return to his island home of Ithaca. *Hyades:* a group of stars. Their rising simultaneously with the sun was supposed to indicate stormy weather.

No. 28, p. 30. *Hornby, Barlow:* the opening batsmen of the Lancashire cricket team in the eighteen-eighties.

No. 30, p. 31. The poem was written about Maud Gonne, a leader of Irish revolutionary action.

No. 32, p. 32. *Mammon:* the god of wealth. The name was used by mediaeval writers for the evil spirit of covetousness.

No. 35, p. 34. *The Battle of Flodden:* fought in Northumberland in 1513. King James IV of Scotland was defeated and killed by the English forces under the Earl of Surrey.

Nos. 39, 40, p. 37. In the course of his wanderings after the fall of Troy, Ulysses and his companions were endangered by the Sirens—the three sea-nymphs who lured sailors to destruction by their song. On another occasion they came to a land inhabited by people who fed on the lotos—a fruit which caused those who ate it to lose all desire to return to their native land.

No. 45, p. 39. *Sir John Franklin* and his companions lost their lives in the ill-fated polar expedition which set out in 1845 to discover the North-West Passage.

No. 59, p. 44, *the Seven Sleepers' den:* according to legend, seven Christian youths sought refuge from the Decian persecution (A.D. 250) in a cave in Mount Celion. There they slept for 230 (or according to some accounts 309) years.

No. 61, p. 46, *the Phoenix:* see note to Nos. 230, 231.

No. 63, p. 46. Dr. Faustus, by his magic art, has conjured up the spirit of Helen of Troy. He imagines that for her sake he will be inspired to perform deeds equal to those of her lover Paris in the Trojan war.
Ilium: Troy.

No. 66, p. 48. *slit so yerne:* slideth (passes away) so quickly.

No. 91, p. 57. *Burd Helen:* in the ballads 'burd' means 'lady, maiden.'

No. 97, p. 61. *Stygian banks:* the banks of the Styx, the river of Hades, over which the shades of the departed were ferried by Charon.

No. 99, p. 62. The second stanza refers to the mediaeval romance of Tristram and Iseult; the third refers to the story of the love of Zeus (who took the form of a swan) and Leda.

No. 134, p. 77. *the royal saint:* King Henry VI, who founded King's College, Cambridge, in 1441.

No. 138, p. 78. *Praxitelean shapes:* works of the great Greek sculptor Praxiteles (born *c.* 390 B.C.).

No. 142, p. 80. *Dürer's Melancholia:* the 'Melancholia' is one of the most famous of the engravings of Albrecht Dürer (1471–1528), the German painter, draughtsman, and engraver.

No. 153, p. 85. *Orpheus:* according to the myth, he played the lyre with such skill that wild beasts, trees, and rocks came to hear him.

No. 154, p. 85. *David Garrick:* the most distinguished actor and theatrical manager of the mid-eighteenth century; friend of Dr. Johnson, Goldsmith, and Reynolds.

No. 158, p. 87. *Nereides:* sea-nymphs; *yarely:* deftly.

Nos. 163, 164, pp. 89–90. *Elkanah Settle* (1648–1724) and *Thomas Shadwell* (1642?–92) were minor poets and dramatists who incurred the enmity of Dryden. He satirized them under the names of Doeg and Og in the second part of *Absalom and Achitophel.*

No. 166, p. 91. *Baiae:* city near Rome; a favourite watering-place of the Romans in the period of the Empire; *in earlier Sicilian:* a reference to the pastoral poetry of the Sicilian poet Theocritus (3rd century, B.C.).

No. 182, p. 98. *Sappho:* Greek poetess of the seventh century B.C.

No. 194, p. 104. *ferlie:* marvel, wonder; *ilka tett:* each lock; *louted:* bowed; *lily leven:* lovely glade; *brae:* hill-side.

No. 198, p. 108. *syne:* afterwards: *eldritch:* weird, hideous; *aske:* newt; *make:* mate, lover.

No. 208, p. 115, *morrow,* mate. The second stanza alludes to (1) the love of Selene (the Moon) for Endymion, (2) the love of Aphrodite (Venus), the wife of Hephaestus (Vulcan —'the heavenly farrier') for Ares (Mars).

No. 212, p. 117. *Ida:* mountain in Crete, where Zeus was said to have been brought up in a cave.

Fair Nine: the nine Muses—divinities presiding over the arts.

No. 214, p. 118. *Pan:* the Greek god of flocks and shepherds. He loved music and invented the shepherd's flute; *Tmolus:* the god of Mount Tmolus. He decided a musical contest between Pan and Apollo; *Tempe:* a beautiful valley in Northern Thessaly; *Peleon:* a mountain in Thessaly; *Sileni:* satyrs: mythical, half-animal creatures of the forest; *Sylvans:* divinities of the fields and forest; *Nymphs:* female divinities associated with mountains, rivers, and trees; *clasp'd a reed:* the Arcadian nymph Syrinx, when pursued by Pan, fled to a river and was changed into a reed.

No. 215, p. 119. *Ilion (Ilium):* see note to No. 63.

No. 216, p. 119, *gladder:* gladdener. *Citheron:* Chaucer confused Mount Cithaeron, sacred to the Muses, with the island Cythera, where Venus was worshipped.

No. 219, p. 120. *Delphos:* the world-famous temple and oracle of Apollo were at Delphi on the slopes of Mount Parnassus. *Genius:* guardian spirit of the place.

No. 225, p. 123. *Hesperian fables:* stories of the golden apples guarded by the Hesperides. It was one of the labours of Hercules to obtain possession of them. *Pan:* see No. 216; *Graces:* goddesses of grace and beauty; *Hours:* goddesses of the seasons and of the weather; *Proserpin:* Proserpina (Greek Persephone), the daughter of Jupiter (Zeus) and Ceres (Demeter), was found by Pluto (or Dis) while gathering flowers in a meadow near Enna, in Sicily, and was carried off to be made queen of the underworld; *Daphne:* a beautiful pleasure garden near Antioch in Syria by the river Orontes; *Castalian spring:* the fountain on Mount Parnassus in which the priestess of the Delphic oracle used to bathe.

Nos. 230, 231, pp. 126–7. *Phoenix:* a fabulous bird. Ancient writers supposed that there was only one of its kind. At the end of its long life it made itself a nest of twigs of spice-trees which it set on fire and so burnt itself alive. From its ashes came forth another phoenix.

Keyes, with Darley's poem as his starting-point, took the Phoenix as a symbol of human pride which has to be consumed.

No. 263, p. 140. *Maeotis:* the ancient name of the Sea of Azov.

No. 276, p. 147. *Ruth:* in the Old Testament story Ruth, a woman of the Moabites, gleaned corn in the fields of Boaz and became his wife.

No. 285, p. 151. *Proserpina:* see note to No. 225.

No. 326, p. 172. The first line is quoted from Bishop Andrewes. The names at the end of the poem are those of imaginary men of different types thought of as emerging from childhood as described in the poem.

No. 330, p. 175. *Catullus:* Roman love-poet (87–54? B.C.).

No. 331, p. 175. *hogo:* a high or piquant flavour (Fr. haut-goût). *Post mortem nulla voluptas:* after death there is no pleasure.

No. 335, p. 178. *Charon:* see note to No. 97.

No. 340, p. 180. *Friar Bacon's brazen head:* the story of the magic head of brass made by Friar Bacon is told in Robert Greene's comedy *Friar Bacon and Friar Bungay* (1594).

No. 379, p. 196. The last stanza was excluded by Gray from the published poem.

No. 382, p. 198. *kellis:* caps; netted headdresses.

No. 386, p. 200. *Academe:* the Academy was the school near Athens where Plato taught philosophy· *The Attic bird:* the nightingale; *Artaxerxes:* King of Persia.

No. 398, p. 204. *Pompey:* Gnaeus Pompeius, the Roman general who was defeated by Julius Caesar at Pharsalia (48 B.C.) and soon afterwards murdered in Egypt.

No. 403, p. 207. *The Earl of Shaftesbury* (Achitophel) was the principal object of attack in Dryden's political satire; his party had attempted to exclude the Duke of York from the succession to the throne and to put the Duke of Monmouth in his place.

No. 404, p. 208. *George Villiers,* second Duke of Buckingham (Zimri), had offended Dryden by introducing references to him in his satirical play *The Rehearsal* (1672).

No. 405, p. 209. *Atticus:* the name under which Pope satirized his former friend, Joseph Addison, the essayist.

No. 406, p. 210. *Eva Gore-Booth and Con Markievicz:* daughters of Sir Henry Gore-Booth, of Lissadell, Co. Sligo. Constance, Countess Markievicz (1868–1927) was an Irish patriot and leader of the Republican movement.

No. 419, p. 218. *Medea:* daughter of Aeetes, King of Colchis. She was a sorceress; *Argus:* called 'the all-seeing' because of his many eyes. He was put to sleep and killed by Hermes.

No. 424, p. 220. *Servants of Man:* each stanza begins with a question put by sceptical spectators to pilgrims devoted to the Goddess Liberty; the rest of the stanza gives the pilgrims' reply.

No. 434, p. 224. *grise:* step; *wappen'd:* worn out: *spitalhouse:* hospital.

No. 442, p. 228. This sonnet, written in 1655, refers to the terrible massacre ordered in that year by Charles Emmanuel II, Duke of Savoy and Prince of Piedmont, of his Protestant subjects the Waldenses or Vaudois. *Babylonian woe:* the Puritans gave the name 'Babylon' to the Papal city of Rome (with allusion to the Book of Revelation).

No. 447, p. 231. *seel:* close up.

No. 460, p. 235. The first stanza is from the First Edition, and the other two are from the Fourth Edition.

No. 465, p. 238. *there:* where.

No. 477, p. 242. *Jacob came clothed,* etc. See Book of Genesis, chap. 27.

No. 478, p. 243. *much and lite:* much and little, i.e. great and small, rich and poor; *despitous:* scornful; *dangerous:* difficult to please; *digne:* haughty; *snybben:* reprove; *spiced:* over-scrupulous.

No. 482, p. 245. *Lente, lente,* etc.: run slowly, slowly, horses of the night.

No. 491, p. 250. *glede:* kite; *xiphias:* sword-fish.

I

266

GEORGE ALLEN & UNWIN LTD
London: 40 Museum Street, W.C.1

Auckland: Haddon Hall, City Road
Sydney, N.S.W.: Bradbury House, 55 York Street
Cape Town: 58–60 Long Street
Bombay: 15 Graham Road, Ballard Estate, Bombay 1
Calcutta: 17 Chittaranjan Avenue, Calcutta 13
New Delhi: Munshi Niketan, Kamla Market, Ajmeri Gate, New Delhi 1
Karachi: Haroon Chambers, South Napier Road, Karachi 2
Toronto: 91 Wellington Street West
Sao Paulo: Avenida 9 de Julho 1138–Ap. 51

by Gilbert Thomas

POEMS: 1912–1919

5s. net

The poems in this volume are selected from the author's previous books of verse, for which, though several of them are out of print, the public still asks. A number of pieces, not hitherto collected, are added.

SELECTED POEMS OLD AND NEW

7s. 6d. net

Leading poets and critics of Mr. Thomas's poetry have acclaimed it as giving fresh vitality to traditional forms and to the enduring values underlying all change, and have declared some of it to be 'permanent.' This volume, long overdue, contains a selection from the poems of forty years, including many now assembled for the first time.

WILLIAM COWPER AND THE EIGHTEENTH CENTURY

New Revised Edition   16s. net

' "The poet, though little aware of the fact was a sensitive instrument, touched by a wind that had begun to sweep across Europe." A brilliant epigram from a brilliant book, it sums up what is delightfully expanded in the other three hundred pages.' *Scottish Guardian*

by Alun Lewis

HA! HA! AMONG THE TRUMPETS

Second Impression   Cr. 8vo.   5s. net

'That he was a true poet . . . and that his death was a
loss to literature. No better verse than this has . . . come
out of the war.' *News Chronicle*

RAIDER'S DAWN

Sixth Impression   Cr. 8vo.   3s. 6d. net

'A selective economy in accurate descriptions; a sudden,
but never incongruous, shifting of the angle of vision;
sustained thought lit by flashes of control of metre . . .
and above all a persistence of poetic vision. . . .' *Dublin
Magazine*

THE LAST INSPECTION AND OTHER STORIES

Third Impression   Cr. 8vo.   7s. 6d. net

'A serious writer, using courage, sympathy and humour
for his critical interpretation of life in the army.' *The
Spectator*

IN THE GREEN TREE

La. Cr. 8vo.   8s. 6d. net

'Remarkable evocation of atmosphere—we feel the
jungle about us, the heat, the sweat, the flies, the lurking
hostility of the villagers, the sense of being lost in an
alien world.' JAMES LAVER (*B.B.C.*)

by Henry Compton

KINDRED POINTS

Cr. 8vo.   7s. 6d. net

'He is a poet of simplicity. His work is delightful to read aloud.' *Birmingham Mail*

'His forthright style, pleasantly free from obscurities of thought and imagery, commands respect by its sincere and enlightened tone.' *Liverpool Daily Post*

'A sensitive artist gifted with strong lyrical fire.' *Plymouth Western Morning News*

'Of singular beauty and appeal.' *Edinburgh Evening News*

by J. A. K. Thomson

CLASSICAL INFLUENCES ON ENGLISH POETRY

La. Cr. 8vo.   15s. net

In his previous book *The Classical Background of English Literature* Professor Thomson made an estimate of the influence exerted upon our literature by the ancient classics. He found it impossible, within the limits of a single book, to illustrate by actual quotation the points made. In *Classical Influences on English Poetry* he sets out to remedy this deficiency, so far as the poets are concerned.

GEORGE ALLEN AND UNWIN LTD